DATE DUE

The Music of

DMITRI SHOSTAKOVICH

The Symphonies

In the same series
edited by DEREK ELLEY and produced by The Tantivy Press
(General Editor: Peter Cowie)

The Music of Joseph Haydn: The Symphonies
The Music of Johannes Brahms
The Music of Johann Sebastian Bach: The Choral Works
The Music of W. A. Mozart: The Symphonies

Forthcoming
The Music of Pyotr Tchaikovsky
The Music of Richard Wagner: The Ring and Parsifal
The Music of Anton Bruckner

THE MUSIC OF DMITRI
SHOSTAKOVICH
THE SYMPHONIES

ROY BLOKKER
with
ROBERT DEARLING

The Tantivy Press/London

Fairleigh Dickinson University Press
Rutherford • Madison • Teaneck

© 1979 by Associated University Presses, Inc.

The Tantivy Press
Magdalen House
136–148 Tooley Street
London SE1 2TT, England

Associated University Presses, Inc.
Cranbury, New Jersey 08512, U.S.A.

ISBN: 0-8386-1948-7
Library of Congress Catalogue Card No.: 78-68623

Cover design by Dreja Hoad Associates
based on an original conception by Mike Carney

Set in 11pt Pilgrim by Five Arches Press (Wales)
and printed in the United States of America

To
the memory of
DMITRI SHOSTAKOVICH

Contents

Acknowledgements

I wish to thank those whose help and encouragement gave me the strength to finish this work, so valuable to my own essence yet so difficult to conceive.

Thanks, first and foremost, go to Mr. Robert Dearling, whose close collaboration on the musical and discographical sections of this book has been both stimulating and of invaluable worth.

Thanks also to Mr. Derek Elley, without whose confidence at an early stage this book would never have reached its final form.

Thanks also go to Mr. Boris Schwarz for the use of material from his book, "Music and Musical Life in Soviet Russia 1917–1970," and to the Philosophical Library for the use of material from Ivan Martinov's book, "Shostakovich: The Man and His Works."

Special thanks must go to Mr. Brad Engel and the people at Angel Records, Los Angeles, whose generosity in providing photographs came at a time when the work seemed at an impasse. Their act provided fresh inspiration and encouragement, and I shall not soon forget them.

We should also like to acknowledge the help of Miss Lessia Dyakivska, a member of the editorial staff of "The Ukrainian Review" in London, for her prompt assistance with information concerning Babi Yar.

All musical examples from Symphonies Nos. 1, 8, 9, 10, 13, 14 and 15 are used by kind permission of Anglo-Soviet Music Press Ltd. (for the British Commonwealth—excluding Canada—and South Africa) and G. Schirmer, Inc. (for U.S.A. and Canada).

Finally, to Diane, my wife, I give my sincerest thanks for hours of patience and valuable criticism that made, I hope, a gentleman from a monster.

Editorial Preface

This series is specifically designed to explore the sound of each composer as his most distinctive feature, and, to this end, recognises the equally important role that recordings now play in musical life. Footnotes throughout the main text contain critical references to such recordings when it is felt that they clarify or highlight the composer's intentions. In the Appendix, these and other recommended recordings are re-grouped in a mostly factual listing of catalogue numbers, performance details and any divergencies from the composer's expressed wishes.

Since the aim of the series is to clarify each composer's sound, particularly for the non-specialist, this approach should prove doubly rewarding: treating concert music as a living rather than an academic entity and showing the virtues and faults of its reflection through Twentieth-century ears.

"Kiss . . . but spit"
(Russian proverb after Pushkin)

Introduction

This book is not a history or a biography. It is the study of a composer's music, specifically his symphonic output. Among Twentieth-century composers Dmitri Shostakovich was a master of the symphonic form. American composer George Antheil once wrote to a friend that he felt too many composers treated the symphonic form shabbily as a mere vehicle for quick recognition and identification, but for Shostakovich Antheil had praise. He wrote, "When, in my letter of yesterday, I spoke about Bruckner, Sibelius, Shostakovich, I meant that in my estimation these three men more than any others continued the line of the great symphonies, and that whatever else may be said against them, they always shot at the stars and attempted to progress music beyond the point at which the last had taken it."

Shostakovich composed fifteen symphonies, a total exceeded only by his countryman Nikolay Myaskovsky, American Alan Hovhaness and Briton Havergal Brian, among noteworthy modern composers. Yet Shostakovich the artist is little appreciated and little heralded in the West. Interest in his music grows among a limited following, and the fact that he was Russian prejudices the ears of many listeners. The task of this book is to better establish his importance to music. Shostakovich should rank as a major voice in the history of the Twentieth-century symphony.

As important as the musical output is the nature of the man. The life of Shostakovich is a study in courage, and that story should be told. It is a story of success and approval against great odds. Music is unalterably bound up with the events around a composer, and he is a rare artist who can divorce himself from his environment—rare but of questionable value. Shostakovich's life and music often act as a barometer of his very volatile environment, Russia under the Soviet state.

This political aspect of Shostakovich's music cannot be ignored. For decades other composers and critics have debated the degree of expressive freedom in Russia for men such as Shostakovich. They invariably wondered what kind of music Shostakovich would have written had he left Russia and settled in Britain or America. Because he chose to stay in Russia, how he himself related to a repressive regime takes on added importance in understanding the man and his music.

Thus, I have written a book which is an appreciation of both his world of beauty and his struggle to find the way to express that world freely.

Shostakovich the Man

Dmitri Dmitriyevich Shostakovich was born in St. Petersburg (now Leningrad) on September 25, 1906 (new calendar). Even as a young boy he showed a remarkable talent and skill in music. When he was five years old his mother took him and his two sisters to see the opera *Tsar Saltan's Fairy Tales (Skazka o tsarye Saltanye)* by Rimsky-Korsakov. The next day young Shostakovich could recite almost the entire score for his bewildered parents—memorised from one hearing. His parents knew then that if he were still interested in music when he grew older he would have a talent to cultivate.

Shostakovich's parents were an interesting pair. His father was born in Siberia of parents in virtual exile. The elder Shostakovich earned the right to study at St. Petersburg University, and settled in that city. There he met Sonya, Dmitri's mother, through his association with Sonya's radical brother. Sonya, especially brilliant in the musical arts and the piano, was enrolled at the Conservatory of Music at the time; her family had also come from Siberia, where her father had been an overseer for mining interests. Sonya and Dmitri Shostakovich Sr. married in 1903. Sonya began giving piano lessons. She believed that art meant hard work and concentrated effort for those willing and able to pursue it, and she always encouraged such a calling for anyone who was ready. In her own son Dmitri she soon found her best pupil. She held off until 1916, when Dmitri was ten, before starting lessons on the piano. He learned them easily and performed them well, even improvising on them for her entertainment. He had fun with his lessons. The parents elected not to push their son, wishing him to keep his childhood as long as possible, but music rapidly became his life and his language. Later that year Shostakovich enrolled in a private school at Shidlovsky. These were special schools for children of radical or intellectual parents, set up as one of the reforms granted by Tsar Nikolay II after the 1905 Revolution. He was simultaneously enrolled at the Glyasser Music School to study piano under M. Glyasser. There he quickly demonstrated skill and potential, earning his teacher's affection.

Up until this point the events of a world at war stayed outside the Shostakovich home. Shostakovich *père* earned promotion during the war and became commercial manager of Promet, a munitions factory; he earned more pay and had the use of two cars, one for official business and one for his family—all this while the Russian soldier was lucky to get one single bullet to use on any given day. The people on the home front were not aware of such ludicrous inadequacies for some time. Sonya Shostakovich continued to earn money with her piano tutoring. The deaths and sicknesses of relatives and friends touched their lives, but in general the war was kind to the Shostakovich household.

By 1917 the temperament of all Russia had changed. When the so-called democratic revolution took place it was welcomed throughout the nation. Even young Shostakovich pleaded with his mother to march with the throng in celebration. Engulfed by the festivities, he composed a "Hymn to Liberty." The exuberance, however, soon wore off and the façade fell apart; the bloodless revolution soon became a bloodbath taking unreasonable directions. The war effort worsened every day. Young Shostakovich witnessed the change first-hand when he saw a policeman brutally kill a small boy suspected of stealing; the incident would later become an episode in his Second Symphony. His mixed emotions prompted another composition which he called "Funeral March for the Victims of the Revolution." Everyone around him said and hoped that the revolution would succeed and the war would stop. Still another composition was called "Revolutionary Symphony." All were early and juvenile attempts, but impressed those who heard them. None was ever written down.

That same spring Shostakovich gave his first performance as part of a school piano recital at Glyasser. Shostakovich appeared last and played Handel's Largo. He was considered the highlight of the recital because of his simple ability to tune his feelings into the interpretation

—not a reading but something more, a quality necessary for a great concert pianist. But at eleven years old he was not considered ready for the Conservatory. In July the abortive first Bolshevik Revolution prompted Shostakovich to require a crash-course from his parents on what revolution meant. He was confused and uncertain as to whom to support. In October the final revolution came, soon followed by the one thing that the democrats could not accomplish but that the people wanted most of all, peace at Brest-Litovsk in March 1918.

In that year both Shostakovich and his older sister passed the necessary examinations and entered the St. Petersburg, now renamed Petrograd, Conservatory of Music. Shostakovich soon composed a *Scherzo* and *Eight Preludes* for piano. Alexandr Glazunov, himself a renowned composer and teacher to such men as Sergey Prokofiev and Nikolay Myaskovsky, heard the works. He saw in them the great potential of the young Shostakovich and sent the boy to study pianoforte and composition under the great master of piano, Professor Maximilian Steinberg. Studies at the conservatory and at regular school, and life at home, went on without event during the next few years. The new Bolshevik government fought a civil war, resisted interference from the angry West and was busy trying to rebuild its domain. War-torn and economically destitute as Russia was, her leaders still recognised the importance of art to the people and did nothing to discourage the continuation of education. They even budgeted what limited funds could be spared to the schools, universities and conservatories, hoping to help those students in greatest need.

On February 24, 1922, after a week's illness, Shostakovich's father died. With his death the Shostakovich family began to feel the strains of the U.S.S.R.'s depressed economy personally. The elder Shostakovich had taken a job with the Soviet government, but upon his death there were no benefits for the widowed Sonya: she had to take a job as a typist in another government agency in addition to her piano lessons. When grief gave way to normalcy the children continued their musical studies. Shostakovich actually abandoned his regular education, saying, "I just can't concentrate on figures, my head is too full of sounds."

Shostakovich the student composed several smaller pieces, most of them for practice. Included were a work called *Soldier* and his *Three Fantastic Dances*, which he wrote for his younger sister, then an aspiring ballerina. *Three Fantastic Dances* would become his first published work, but Shostakovich tore up most of the practice pieces in a rage prompted by self-doubt some time before he sat down to write the First Symphony. After completing his training as a pianist in 1923, he was found to have tuberculosis. An operation on the cervical gland failed to arrest the disease; a second operation and a trip to a sanatorium were somehow paid for. He seemed to improve, but there was not enough money to continue the treatments, so they were abandoned. Shostakovich returned home and tried to renew his studies in composition.

January 1924 was the low point. Shostakovich was in bed with bronchitis on top of the tuberculosis, and his mother had collapsed from over-work and malaria. Her job was not kept open for her return. Shostakovich's older sister provided the only financial support by giving music lessons, and also kept house as best she could, running herself ragged in the bargain. His younger sister was going through a difficult teenage stage with which no one else could help her; consequently, she was no help to them and in fact a constant irritant. Shostakovich's eye-glasses were broken: without them the student could barely see, let alone study, but there was no money to spare to have them fixed. In this way Shostakovich came to know the poverty and suffering common to the Russian people at the time of their government's birth.

By the winter of 1924/25 things looked better. The elder sister started teaching not only privately but also at a ballet school. Sonya secured a new job on low pay. Shostakovich himself continued again at the conservatory, but his return was not pleasant. Petty teenage rivalries among the students placed him, absent for so long, at a dis-advantage, and the free lessons his professors had arranged for him in the past from government funds and donations were no longer available because of pressures to spread what little there was evenly. Shostakovich wanted to help his family. Because they were all working for his education he wanted to do his part, and to earn money he took a job playing the piano in a local film theatre, accompanying the silent screen for three shows a night. In the middle of winter the customers huddled close together in their furs, their body-heat making the building hot and sticky; when the film was over the manager threw open the doors and the people rushed out as the cold air rushed in. Shostakovich's tuberculosis was aggravated by the conditions, but the job lasted only a short while. This early exposure to the cinema predestined a later long association, during which he would compose music for over three dozen films.

In the midst of that winter Shostakovich began his First Symphony. It was his graduation piece, and he finished it in early 1926. The experts at the conservatory thought highly of the score and felt it should and could be played if somehow the 150 roubles to have copies made for the musicians could be rounded up. Such confidence did the conservatory have that it undertook to pay for the printing fees on Shostakovich's behalf, and Nikolay Malko studied the score in great detail. On May 12, the last concert date of the Leningrad Philharmonic season, the symphony was first performed. It was to be the first of so many dramatic and exciting Shostakovich *premières*. The unknown talent won over every-one. The audience approved of the work so heartily that they called upon the orchestra to encore the Scherzo, and both Shostakovich and conductor Malko were cheered for curtain call after curtain call. The success of the *première* was repeated in Moscow with the composer playing the piano. Shostakovich was praised as an up-and-coming Russian, *Soviet* composer, one worthy to be lined up alongside the masters of any other nation. The Soviet government was quick to notice its *first* truly talented, totally Soviet artist, and was certain to make use of him. This sudden limelight was a sure help to Shostakovich's career, for given his shy nature and quiet, private personality, he might well have been overlooked but for being the right man at the right time.

Critics acclaimed the First Symphony as one of the most complete of all first symphonies. Many critics still make the same observation. A nineteen-year-old boy, a thin and ailing composer-aspirant, had composed a mature, appealing work most noticeable for its confident restraint. The Soviet government paid all expenses for Shostakovich to travel to Berlin to attend the *première* there under the baton of Bruno Walter. Shostakovich became invaluable to the government at the outset of his career: the Soviet leaders cast their lot with him as their first artistic representative, neither party at this point realising how confining the arrangement might become.

Not only were benefits starting to come in from the success of the symphony, but Shostakovich also began to earn the plaudits of an international reputation with the successful introduction of the First in Berlin, later Vienna, and still later in America with Leopold Stokowski conducting. Due to his enormous talent and because a handful of people recognised that talent and promoted it, Dmitri Shostakovich had arrived.

*

Soon after the success of the First Symphony Shostakovich entered a piano recital contest in Warsaw and among a large field he won an honourable mention. In other recitals around Russia he won consistent praise: there was no question that he was a master of the keyboard, but he felt it was time to make a choice between composing and performing. It was a difficult choice. Shostakovich wanted to apply himself fully to only one facet of music and do that well; he did not believe he could be successful at both simultaneously, in the manner of Liszt. It seemed that either route he chose would prove financially lucrative, and he chose composing, even though his First Symphony would be hard to follow. Shostakovich actually abandoned composition for a time after his graduation from the conservatory. For eighteen months he did little else besides study the music of others, to broaden his perspective and increase his knowledge of musical literature. While studying within the conservatory he got little exposure, but now he was free to explore.

The music he studied was music from the West, which Russians could now hear for the first time since the Revolution.

A cultural thaw began in 1924, a year after Lenin's death. This thaw spread to all aspects of the arts, while revolutionaries and artists alike sought to redefine their own culture and significance. The doors to the West were thrown open, and culture-starved Russians flocked to the *premieres* of such works as Alban Berg's *Wozzeck*. They heard Mahler and Bruckner for the first time, as well as Paul Hindemith, Darius Milhaud, Arthur Honegger, Ernst Křenek and others. Hindemith, Berg and Milhaud were among several who were invited to Russia to attend and perform their own concerts. For Shostakovich this exposure came late, for he did not start studying these composers until after his graduation in 1926. Shostakovich felt held back by scholastic traditions and he wanted to explore, but both Alexandr Glazunov and Max Steiner opposed such exploration within the conservatory, as they believed the institution had to preserve the classical ideals. Their arch conservatism kept modern ideas on the outside. Soon modernism would be poorly received in Russia as her leaders adopted a stand similar to the conservatory directors, but at this time experimentation was encouraged.

Shostakovich's first modern project was a stunning piece for piano: *Aphorisms (Aforizmy)*.* He followed that with his Second Symphony, commissioned to celebrate the Tenth Anniversary of the Revolution. It is ironic that the composer could write this work as an experiment while using themes in a choral ending that were strictly ideological, strictly what the Soviet leaders felt would be ideal in Russian art. The idiom was modern, the message party-line. The score used revolutionary poetry and music in a somewhat obvious attempt to emulate Beethoven, another spokesman for the Revolution of Man. Shostakovich, now twenty, was branching out. His experiments were well received by other modernists, many of whom were after two things: realism, and newness for the sake of newness as a symbol of the revolution. The opera, *The Nose (Nos)*, was the highlight of Shostakovich's experimentation. In it he presented a score with an incredible plot and wild, intendedly humorous and even banal orchestral combinations, in which he amply demonstrated his command of the orchestra.† During this period money

---

* Though stunning and brilliant, the work was *later* seen as ultra-modern and decadent by Soviet critics. At the time the critics, themselves pro-modern, loved it.

† Critics were to lampoon *The Nose* in a short while, calling it an attempt to negate opera as a musical form. The plot is fantastic, complicated and with many a *non sequitur*, following the main character as he searches for his nose, accidentally severed by a barber; the scenes that trace his story are an intended social satire written in merriment. The staging (for seventy-eight participants) was both strange and difficult, and the music, although engaging and showing the composer's mastery of the orchestra and flair for the grotesque, was considered peculiar. After some initial success, the message of the opera was lost and the score ultimately failed.

started coming into the Shostakovich household from benefits drawn from his First Symphony and the commissions being offered for film and theatre scores and the symphonies. The Shostakovich household was beginning to feel comfortable once again when the Second Symphony—the first of his experiments with any widespread success—was premiered on November 6, 1927, in Leningrad under Malko.

In the late Twenties Shostakovich began a close association with film music, using that arena as a testing ground for his ideas throughout his career. Film commissions would also provide a steady source of work and income even when his "important" music was in official disfavour. In 1928 Josef Stalin and the Soviet Central Committee began taking a more active interest in the direction of Soviet music. The experimentation from 1924 onwards had been a search for a Soviet art-form, but near the end of the decade no solid form or pattern was forthcoming on any artistic front. The government had its own ideas even if the artists did not, and the leaders saw only chaotic activity: they began cracking down on Western influences, which they saw as disruptive and splintering, and substituted an ideal of Soviet realism which was more heroic than realistic. They intended that Russian artists should depict in clear terms the strength and accomplishments of the Soviet state, which meant that the symphony itself was in jeopardy in favour of popular operas and songs. For a time anything intellectual or in any way beyond the grasp of the people was unwelcome.

For Shostakovich this period was one of pressure, as he had to keep pace with his commissions and seek to find a middle ground between composing music with mass appeal and music that would elevate the listener closer to his own level. He wanted to satisfy the public on one hand and create lasting beauty on the other. The struggle to find a way to do both together filled him with self-consciousness and doubt. It was not until 1937 that he found a viable synthesis with his Fifth Symphony.

In 1930 the Third Symphony appeared, his first attempt at a fusion between the symphony and Soviet realism, as well as his first consolidation of ideas. Shostakovich's reputation called for him to make many public appearances. He was a living advertisement of the goodness and wealth of the Soviet state. He also was working hard on new ballet and film scores. While recovering from an appendectomy he met Nina Varzar and planned to marry her, but neither family would hear of it, temporarily at least. Under these pressures and his own drive Shostakovich grew more reserved, more introverted and restrained. He began to rely on music as his major language, and it met with continued success. The next four years saw consolidation on all fronts. In 1930/31 Shostakovich composed two ballet suites, *The Age of Gold (Zolotoy vyek)* and *The Bolt (Bolt)*. As ballets they were not successful, being considered little more than revues, but the suites he derived from them were considered charming and fun and became big concert hits. Even when lightness in music was considered a sinful travesty of a classicist's talents—beer hall music belonging in beer halls—Shostakovich strove to write gay, satirical, joking music. He incorporated such moments in his most serious projects. ". . . I hoped to write good, entertaining music," he once said, "which would be pleasant or even amusing. . . It gives me pleasure to see my audience laugh or even smile." In 1932 he married Nina Varzar privately and presented both families with a *fait accompli* which they reluctantly accepted. Sonya Shostakovich came to live with her son and new daughter-in-law until Shostakovich could set her up in her own flat in 1935. In 1934, after a long period of planning, Shostakovich announced a scheme to compose a tetralogy of operas in praise of Russian womanhood which would take ten years to complete. The first of the four operas was premiered on January 22, 1934, and was entitled *Lady Macbeth of Mtsensk (Ledi Makbet mtsenskovo uyezda)*, based on a short story by Nikolay Leskov. The work was an immediate success everywhere: the government, just recently recognised by the United States, wanted to use the opera as a piece of goodwill propaganda to promote the new attitudes of the Soviet abroad; Artur Rodziński called it one of the most important works of the Twentieth century and presented it in America, where audiences of the day liked the stark manner in which Shostakovich presented his story. For two years the opera was a success at home and throughout Europe, where its suggestiveness made it appear charming and refreshingly daring; nowhere it played were the critics silent about the work.

Lightning struck Shostakovich suddenly on January 28, 1936, two full years after the opera's first performance. "Pravda," the official Party newspaper, published an article that called the opera confusion instead of music, saying that the composer had let the compliments of the past go to his head and thus had forgotten himself and presented unworthy music, not because of a lack of talent but because he was trying to reject operatic form. Such terms as "leftist," "formalist," "cacophony" and "musical chaos" were applied. "Pravda" felt that the story was given a significance it did not deserve: the setting was vulgar, sexual and violent - blatantly and without taste. The opera was decadent. One critic said Shostakovich had developed a new type of music, "pornophony."* A week later Shostakovich's ballet score, *The Limpid Brook (Svyetli ruchey)*, was also attacked, a move which effectively

---

* It is interesting that this particular critic was a Westerner. While the Soviets looked upon the opera as a symbol of Western decadence the West saw the same opera as a sign of Russian corruption.

destroyed his career as a ballet composer.* The "Pravda" article of February 6 stated that the composer showed his lack of concern for national songs, and thus national heritage and purpose. Both "Pravda" articles were unsigned, lending them the credo of being formal government declarations. Shostakovich was in deep trouble, and soon others joined the bandwagon of criticising the vulnerable composer: he was boycotted and ostracised; few sided with him; Sergey Prokofiev's name was linked with his as Prokofiev's own reputation as an *enfant terrible* was recalled. Stalin intervened personally on Prokofiev's behalf and told the critics to leave the dean of composers alone, and Prokofiev for his part continued to speak for Shostakovich. The Moscow Composers' Union held heated debates whether or not to denounce the composer of *Lady Macbeth*. Telling Shostakovich that he had sacrificed ideological and emotional content for the pursuit of new sounds via cheap orchestral tricks, the Union decided *not* to drop him from their roster. Instead they would help him find his way back.

Prokofiev once stated that he wrote music of two types: one for the masses and one for posterity. Shostakovich had been trying to fuse the two into one, and although his attempts did not fall short of his own expectations, they fell short of his government's and he was attacked. He seemed to be a slave to two masters, both art and the state, as he found out sadly in 1936. Even his best friend stepped away from him: Ivan Sollertinsky, a brilliant music critic, was the man who had introduced much of the modern music to Shostakovich that the composer had hungered for after 1926, but now Sollertinsky criticised Shostakovich's music along with the others, though admittedly only after being placed under tremendous pressure. This was the time of the purges throughout Russia, from farmers in the Ukraine to political figures in Moscow. Shostakovich's position was rightly taken as a warning to everyone else to tread softly and agree with the government. Sollertinsky was branded "the bard of formalism" and threatened with the spectre of permanent unemployment. Instead he bent. Shostakovich forgave his friend's weakness at that crucial moment. When Sollertinsky was killed in 1944 at the age of forty-one Shostakovich dedicated his Second Piano Trio to the memory of his friend.

There was a story that Stalin prompted the attack on Shostakovich because, when he first saw *Lady Macbeth of Mtsensk* in 1936, he sat over the thunderous brass section and was almost blasted out of the opera house. Such a story appeals to our image of Stalin, but is doubtful.

---

* The ballet was considered weak and without character. The composer had attempted to depict life on a collective farm or *kolkhoz*, in the Kuban Cossack region, but the music was too superficial for official taste. Subsequently, Shostakovich derived three suites based on this music, showing his personal liking for the score, but only one more ballet came to light—taken from his Eleventh Symphony.

Stalin prided himself on keeping up with art and was particularly fond of opera, so would not have waited two years to see *Lady Macbeth*. Secondly, it is doubtful whether one man alone, even Stalin, could have created a pure policy statement directed against music; the state was largely a government by committee, and although Shostakovich was the target of attack, the causes were elsewhere. State policy established in 1936 called the opera false philosophy. With Fascism abroad and the world antagonistic, the Soviet leaders wanted unity and positivism at home. Art was an expression of unity or disunity depending on what was said: it was not the music but the content of *Lady Macbeth* which promoted disunity in their opinion. The point of the controversy was Katerina as a heroine. To a struggling state she must have seemed a parasite not to be encouraged, and the Soviet leaders wanted positive art that would promote a happy Soviet people. Shostakovich's opera was depressing and intellectual, albeit entertaining. It was realism but not Soviet realism.

The 1936 purge of Shostakovich was inevitable. When Stalin's close friend Sergey Kirov was assassinated on December 1, 1934, the shock-wave started a bloody purge of Stalin's supposed enemies, among them some of the Party's most respected men. The fact that Kirov was assassinated in Leningrad, Shostakovich's home town, made Stalin and Kirov's successor Andrey Zhdanov especially wary of that city. The Central Committee clamped down on anything that might be even a small threat or challenge to their authority. They were already certain that war with Germany was inevitable and that the Western appeasers were promoting it. Challenging his leaders' authority was the furthest thing from Shostakovich's mind but, as Shostakovich was alone under attack, Russia was alone in the world. She lashed out protectively on all fronts. The fact that *Lady Macbeth* was composed by Russia's native son made action against him imperative, and to dare to attack him showed that the government really meant business. The duty of the artist, as the government saw things now, was simple: build confidence and solidarity and love for the fatherland, right or wrong. Be heroic.* An example was made of Shostakovich. The Soviet government was more interested in scores like Prokofiev's 1938 heroic cantata from the film *Alexandr Nevsky*. Later in 1936 *Lady Macbeth of Mtsensk* was banned as the first act of preparation for the inevitable war with Germany.

---

* A somewhat lesser opera, Ivan Dzerzhinsky's *And Quiet Flows the Don (Tikhi Don)*, was used as an example of positive art. It depicted the sturdy Cossack stock in heroic terms, and was seen as an attempt to soothe the ruffles after the bloody farming purges had been settled. Ironically, the opera was written with the advice of and *dedicated* to Shostakovich, who saw great potential in Dzerzhinsky. The opera was awarded the Stalin Prize.

The arguments against Shostakovich were ridiculous. Prokofiev expressed his great fear of this one-victim purge; the warning was clear. Shostakovich himself believed in the works that were attacked but remained silent under the barrage, since he knew that he had sincerely tried to serve his government's purposes all along. But now he faced harsh criticism, threats of total ostracism from the ranks of the Composers' Union; even political exile was a possibility. He would be vindicated in 1963 when the opera, renamed *Katerina Izmaylova*, would be revived and hailed as a true masterpiece.* The 1936 case against him was a prime example of a totalitarian government's power and strength over its people. For Shostakovich the question became what to do when you believe in your government and its progress but it attacks you for yours—the most difficult question the young man had to face. He could have run away, but instead set out to redefine his own role in Soviet art, to see if in fact he was in error or if his vision of purpose was correct for him. The composer remained silent—for a time.

For two years Shostakovich's name virtually disappeared from the concert hoardings. To prevent more controversy he withdrew his brooding, elaborate Fourth Symphony after its tenth rehearsal; it would not be heard until 1961. Good news came in the form of a baby daughter, Galya, born that spring. Shostakovich took up teaching duties at the conservatory and quietly began planning the Fifth Symphony, keeping his feelings to himself. He never completed another serious opera or a ballet. He did some work on film scores, which often served as a refuge from the critical eye of the government,† but most of his silent effort went towards the score that would win him permanent fame. Russian biographers said the 1936 Decrees put the composer back on the right road; Western critics said his inventiveness was destroyed. Neither were strictly correct—Shostakovich would probably have gone the same way with or without the intervention of a paranoid, frightened government.

*

Few works in the history of music had as strong an impact on audiences or on the position between patron and artist as did the Fifth Symphony. The score, as can be seen now, was a more concise expression of the same basic ideas used in the withdrawn Fourth Symphony—in other words, the Fourth matured. Shostakovich subtitled the score "A Soviet Artist's Reply to Just Criticism," a title not to be ignored, but upon hearing the work none could doubt Shostakovich had not changed

---

* Unfortunately, it is seldom heard outside Russia.
† In fact, Shostakovich would be warned in 1948 not to "retire" completely into film music.

but matured: the score was not Soviet realism but Shostakovich realism; it was the composer's answer to whatever criticism of the past two years that *was* just.

The symphony was premiered on November 21, 1937, in Leningrad under Yevgyeni Mravinsky, and was a great success to a capacity audience. It was successful everywhere it was played—Shostakovich had earned his way back into the good graces of his government and its leaders with a positive masterpiece. By the time of the *première* Russia was experiencing another, though limited, cultural thaw. Internal strife had somewhat lessened and unity programmes were taking effect. The temper of the times had modified and the political climate had grown more liberal. There were plans for a new constitution in the offing. Sergey Prokofiev had remained the dean of Soviet music and himself kept defending Shostakovich. Even the original attacks on Shostakovich's work had left him a way out: they blamed not his talent but his use of that talent and the formalism that led him astray. The Fifth Symphony was taken as a sign of his reformation, and the government was probably as grateful to have an acceptable work offered as Shostakovich was to have it accepted. Audiences in Russia loved the score; around the world audiences and critics saw in it the promise of the First Symphony at last brought to fruition. The Leningrad *première* was only the initial success. From that moment on Shostakovich became one of the top two or three composers in all Russia and never relinquished that position. The score was used as part of the celebrations to commemorate the Twentieth Anniversary of the Revolution. Soon war would make Shostakovich a national hero. Commissions started coming in again on a steady basis, and his duties as a teacher—much to his own surprise—were of benefit to both master and pupils. Shostakovich could love his land freely again, could feel free again. Whereas the opera had come at the wrong time, the symphony had come at the right time, and reaffirmed Shostakovich's image of himself and his role.

The next few years were filled with intellectual activity. Between the Fifth and Sixth Symphonies Shostakovich presented music for five films and wrote his first quartet, opus 49. He would prove to be as much a master of the chamber form as the full orchestra, and would compose fifteen quartets. In 1938 his son Maxim was born. At this point the Shostakovich family was filled with confidence.

In 1939 the Sixth Symphony was premiered and was received coolly only because it was not what Shostakovich had originally announced. He had made plans for a *magnum opus* based on the life and thoughts of Lenin, but instead presented an unassuming, uncomplicated, *pretty* work filled with a playful carnival atmosphere. Shostakovich assured the public that he needed more time to do justice to the grander theme, meanwhile presenting a diversion. He scored another major success less than a year later with his next significant chamber work, the Piano Quintet, opus 57. The quintet was premiered in the Small Hall of the conservatory in Moscow on November 23, 1940, with the Beethoven Quartet joined by Shostakovich himself at the piano. The work followed a long concert programme of chamber works, but the audience, tired and listless at the start, was literally charmed back to life, with the Scherzo and Finale encored. It was a typically successful Shostakovich *première*, the kind of performance and material that led people to expect brilliance and excitement at each successive *première*. The quintet further endeared him to the state, winning Shostakovich the Stalin Prize, First Class, worth 100,000 roubles. The Piano Quintet has retained its reputation as one of its composer's finest works. Apparently Shostakovich set out to compose the Lenin Symphony after the quintet, but he never finished the project.

When Hitler launched his Plan Barbarossa, the invasion of Russia, on June 22, 1941, Leningrad was one of the main targets. Shostakovich was in the city when the Germans reached its outer defences and began the siege of Leningrad in July. No Russian had expected the 1939 Non-Aggression Pact with Germany to stand for very long, but the time that document bought worked to German advantage. Now two hundred Axis divisions were rolling across Russia : Hitler wanted to make an example of Leningrad. Instead the Leningraders gave the world an example of courage and strength, even beauty, in the ugliest circumstances. Shostakovich demonstrated that example to all the world. Using his gift for musical language he created a tribute to his city and to Leningraders' courage—the world's free audiences would hear their story through his work. The stories about the Leningrad Symphony were legend in their day, carrying all the mystique of the voice of victory from the depths of hell. The publicity given the work was incredible. Few pieces of music in all history met with more inspired success, and Shostakovich emerged as a symbol and a national hero.

The history of the score was the most interesting part of all. On the very day of the invasion Shostakovich tried to enlist in the army, but he was rejected, not only because of his poor eyesight but because he was considered a national resource to be kept as safe as possible. In fact, the government in Moscow tried to make Shostakovich leave Leningrad as it became obvious that the city was a target soon to be reached by the enemy. Shostakovich kept refusing to leave. Instead he worked inside the city as a volunteer fireman and in connection with the "Home-Guard Theatre." He wrote patriotic songs and edited new works by other artists in the city. Meanwhile the siege was on. It would last almost 900 days and claim somewhere between 600,000 and 1,000,000 lives. Shostakovich himself told Alexander Werth in 1959 that the figure was actually 900,000. The entire war was personified in the drama of the city, and the spirit of the Allies could be seen in the stubborn spirit of the people of Leningrad. Shostakovich tried to capture that spirit in his Seventh Symphony. Whenever his other duties were not pressing he composed, even during air raids, as if possessed. "The music surged out of me, I could not hold it back," he said later. He worked at incredible speed even for him. By September, when the government finally ordered him to leave the besieged city, he had already completed the first three movements and advance publicity was starting.

The score was completed in December in Kuibyshev, to where Shostakovich and his family had retreated along with many other artists. Under the baton of Samuel Samosud the symphony was first performed there on March 3, 1942, and Samosud also conducted the Moscow *première* later that month. Victor Seroff reported that Shostakovich acted as a man about to be hanged in the days preceding: the excitement must have been unbearable for him, especially after all the build-up given the work—he had given a score expressly to the people of Russia at war, and awaited their approval. It was a daylight concert in Moscow: halfway through the performance a soldier climbed on stage and warned the audience of an impending air-raid, but no one moved. Repeated warnings were not heeded and the symphony was played throughout the alert. Even afterwards the audience refused to take shelter, instead giving a standing ovation to orchestra and composer—and to Leningrad.

The drama attached to the symphony was not confined to Russia. In the United States conductors fought for the privilege of giving the Western *premiere*. Sergei Koussevitzky was most anxious to receive the honour: always highly critical of Russian Communism, he wanted to prove that the Allies were all one and the same now. But concert commitments and pre-arranged programmes conflicted with Koussevitzky's hopes, and Arturo Toscanini finally won the honour.

Interest in the score was phenomenal. The Seventh had become a weapon of propaganda apart from its intrinsic musical value; it had already appealed to millions and would appeal to millions more, but first it had to reach them. With all the intrigue of a secret document, the score was copied on microfilm, the film packed in a small tin and flown from Moscow to Tehran and then driven by car to Cairo. The precious work was then flown across the Sahara to Casablanca, and across the Atlantic via Brazil to the United States. Shortly thereafter Toscanini and the NBC Symphony played the score over the radio to the American nation in July 1942.* Because of its value and message, by and large the symphony was well received by wartime Western audiences, though never with the natural enthusiasm a Russian would

---

* A recording of this event has been issued to the public; see the Recommended Recordings section.

have for a Russian work. Most of the press hailed the patriotism of the music and said that Shostakovich spoke for all mankind.* Koussevitzky conducted the concert *première* of the work at Tanglewood, Massachusetts, to start off the 1942/43 season, during which time the symphony would be played sixty-two times by various orchestras in America.

After the *première* of the Seventh, Shostakovich and his family settled permanently in Moscow when the capital city seemed no longer in danger of attack. Soon communications were restored between Moscow and besieged Leningrad. Shostakovich renewed his teaching duties with those who were left via this communications system. He also composed a few war-oriented works, including a piece for chorus and orchestra entitled *Leningrad*. While working on the first movement of the Seventh he had wanted to add words to the section. Only restraint stopped him, and he was glad of the result, but he fulfilled the need for a choral tribute to Leningrad with this suite, premiered on October 15, 1942.

Shostakovich was now "safe" and tucked away. He spent the militarily decisive summer of 1943 at the "Creative House" of the Union of Soviet Composers, near Ivanovo, fifty miles outside Moscow. There were twenty or so prominent composers like Shostakovich at the House, among them Prokofiev, Myaskovsky, Aram Khachaturyan and Dmitri Kabalevsky. The war effort went on without these people. They had to react to the news that came in. Reports of brutalities by the Germans against Russian civilians as well as soldiers grew in frequency: Shostakovich's Second Trio, op. 67 (1944), was a personal reaction to news of uncovered concentration camps. The Russians were carrying the brunt of the fighting on their own soil, and though the great push to drive the enemy back into Germany had begun after the pivotal triumph at Kursk that spring, the Russian dead kept piling up.

Prompted by frustration and despair, Shostakovich began his Eighth Symphony during the summer of 1943. The product of his labour was an elaborate, brooding score, deeply felt, much better in quality than the Seventh. The Eighth was very close to the mood of the time, filled with sadness and, in the same breath, determination.

As the war drew to a close the composer began plans for a great final symphony of victory, on the lines of Beethoven's Ninth, to

---

* Victor Seroff gave this account of a conversation with Sergey Rakhmaninov on the occasion of the work's American radio première: "Rachmaninoff (*sic*) thought that Shostakovich was very talented, but he hoped that sooner or later Shostakovich would leave Russia so that his creative ability would be free to develop and not remain attached to the tail of ever changing political lines. However, as he spoke of Dmitri Shostakovich, I felt Rachmaninoff's great pride that the music to which millions were listening at the moment came from a Slav like himself." (Seroff, "Rachmaninoff," New York, 1950, pp. 227–8.)

form a wartime trilogy. The Russian government and people expected a grand symphony of summation, surpassing both the Seventh and the Eighth. Shostakovich even began a triumphant opening movement, orchestrated it, then abandoned it, apparently scrapping the entire plan along with it. He could not contrive a score; he did not *feel* the music he was contemplating. It was not until the summer of 1945 that he began what became his Ninth Symphony, and the work was completed that August. He then gave his countrymen *his* celebration of the end of the war.

With his Ninth Symphony Shostakovich presented himself as a man very happy the war was over. In the score there was no political determination, only joy.* Shostakovich was not concerned with another banner for his guaranteed victorious government, and the latter quickly attacked the score, saying that Shostakovich's music "does not reflect the true spirit of the Soviet people." At first audiences were disappointed by the Ninth, but soon they were charmed. The score *did* reflect their true spirit, their festive mood. But the government's disappointment was coupled with the fact that none of the other major composers brought forth a symphony of summation either. The leaders of Russia felt that the country needed a heroic symphony at this juncture: they were not sure that the Russian people, unified by war, would remain unified now that peace and rebuilding were at hand. The arts could, and therefore had to, promote heroic unity and establish in the people the spirit and desire to do the hard work ahead.

The symphony was premiered on November 3, 1945, by the Leningrad Philharmonic, conducted by Yevgyeni Mravinsky. Outside Russia it was premiered in December 1945 at a concert given by the Prague Philharmonic, conducted by Raphael Kubelík. In the United States Koussevitzky held the *première* at Tanglewood. When the Ninth was criticized in Russia Koussevitzky rose to its defence, calling the symphony "one of the most beautiful of our contemporary works."

*

In 1948 Andrey Zhdanov, speaking on behalf of the Central Committee, the hub of the government, launched a vicious attack on all the major composers. The attack had been brewing since the end of the war and, although Shostakovich was a central figure, he was not alone now as he had been twelve years earlier. With Russia's leaders afraid they might lose their hold on the populace and having to cope

---

* Some critics thought the symphony a joke. Some, like Rabinovich (*op. cit.*), over-ideologised the work, trying, as was common, to attach meanings to it that were not there, in defence of their composer.

with the spectre of the United States having—and twice using—the atomic bomb, a tight watch was put over the arts that would not be eased until after Stalin's death. The Zhdanov Decree of 1948 launched the period.

Shostakovich's Ninth began the fire. Nikolay Myaskovsky, then sixty-eight, wrote his Twenty-Fifth Symphony to express his feelings about the end of the war. This score, premiered in 1947, also was no summation of victory but an expression of the serenity of at last being at peace. Then Sergey Prokofiev presented his Sixth Symphony. It was also premiered in 1947 and was universally ill received. Economical in expression and lyric in mood, the Sixth became a focal point for the Zhdanov attack.* At the time Shostakovich was working on a patriotic cantata, but it was slow in coming and the government's leaders remembered other "promises" their favourite son had not kept.

Zhdanov was a strong and well-meaning bureaucrat who felt the need to dabble in the arts. It was largely his doing when Shostakovich was singled out for attack in 1936. Zhdanov had a personal dislike for Shostakovich because he was from Leningrad: he had succeeded Kirov there in 1934 as head of the party after Kirov had been shot, and distrusted the city and its people. Zhdanov could not appreciate Shostakovich's quiet, modest, subtle ways and delicate nature, the very opposite to his own. He was helped by Tikhon Khrennikov, who became Secretary General of the Composers' Union the same year. Khrennikov was an opportunist, a better diplomat than composer, who capitalised on his new position to gain favour and power with Stalin and Zhdanov. Khrennikov specified and elaborated the attacks, heavily singling out Prokofiev, Shostakovich, Myaskovsky, Khachaturyan, Kabalevsky and others in a long list of expertly delineated transgressions, even attacking Stravinsky *in absentia* and at one point referring to Prokofiev as an alien influence astray from the Russian fold. They were all accused of writing confused music, pathologically discordant and occupied by private whims. They were further accused of corrupting the minds of their students.† The government of Russia made a policy statement calling for all composers to write *proletarian music*, music with mass appeal for mass consumption.

Shostakovich was summoned before the committee, along with Prokofiev and the others, to hear the accusations formally read by

---

* What was the trigger for such widespread attack? One account shows that Stalin was angered by the dissonances and loudness of Vano Muradeli's opera, *Great Friendships* (*Velikaya druzhba*). The same argument was used in 1936 and is as unlikely as the story of Stalin's dissatisfaction with *Lady Macbeth of Mtsensk*. At any rate, Muradeli's opera was the first work attacked and the numbers swelled from there. *Great Friendships* was no more than a catalyst; the Soviet Central Committee wanted to declare musical policies.

† This remarkable document is in print and makes fascinating reading. See Slonimsky, N., "Music Since 1900" (New York, 1949), pp. 689–96.

Zhdanov himself. Prokofiev reportedly turned his back while the reading took place and in a clearly audible aside to Shostakovich said, "What do ministers know of music? That is the business of composers." Facing censure and denunciation, most formally apologised for erroneous adventures: Prokofiev, recuperating from a heart attack, apologised in a letter; Shostakovich and many others in public.* Shostakovich said, ". . . I again deviated in the direction of formalism, and began to speak in a language incomprehensible to the people . . . I know that the Party is right . . . I am deeply grateful . . . for all the criticism contained in the Resolution." Alexander Werth observed that the apologies by Shostakovich were "words of a great artist, utterly bewildered by what was happening . . . words of a man—still just over forty—who feels himself crushed and beaten . . ." Shostakovich again felt attacked for doing what he thought best served both his patron and his art. His entire musical output was attacked by also-rans who suddenly had the power of censure: a songwriter named Zakharov, for example, criticised his symphonies, but Shostakovich answered, saying, "It seems to me that he was not right, because there are, in our symphonic music, many great achievements, though there are also faults and failures . . ."

Both the attacks and the apology caused him great sorrow in the five years that followed, before he found expression in his *tour de force*, the Tenth Symphony. Shostakovich entered a period of caution from 1948 to 1953, knowing how carefully all composers would be watched and wanting to avoid any more political controversy at this point. He continued to work on two levels, almost "retiring" into film scores for his "accessible" music while still working on music for posterity in a less publicised way. He still refused to be compromised: he would write film scores and cantatas as long as they were entertaining and not important. He held back his First Violin Concerto under the circumstances, but in chamber works such as the Fourth Quartet (1949) and his magnificent 24 Preludes and Fugues (1950) it was obvious that he

---

*Nikolay Myaskovsky did not apologise at all. Although Zhdanov would die in six months, Khrennikov and others pressed on with the purge. Myaskovsky became a principle victim, and was devastated by the attacks because, though an innovator, he felt close to the goals of Russian nationalism in music. He baulked at the decree and refused to attend the committee meeting, though summoned along with the rest. *In absentia* he was stripped of his professorship. That some of his most prized students, notably Khachaturyan and Kabalevsky, and his best friend, Prokofiev, were also attacked made the moment especially painful for him. But with stubborn courage he refused to apologise. His Twenty-Sixth Symphony was coolly received, but his Cello Sonata of 1949 won a Stalin Prize. His professorship was restored late in 1948 in deference to his age. In 1950 his Twenty-Seventh Symphony, heroic yet soulful, was seen as a major success, an acceptance of Soviet realism. It won Myaskovsky another Stalin Prize—posthumously, for he had died on August 9, 1950, of cancer, twenty-five years to the day before Shostakovich.

had not given in musically. In 1958 the post-Stalin Central Committee would declare that the February 1948 Zhdanov Proclamation was too harsh towards several of the composers listed. Shostakovich was specifically mentioned. Shostakovich himself had just pleaded with the Second Composers' Congress in 1957 to allow a more liberal atmosphere of discussion between musical liberals and conservatives. The 1958 repeal was a government sanction of such tolerance, spearheaded by Nikita Krushchev.

But that was ten years off. For five years Shostakovich waited patiently, taking up duties as a spokesman for peace. After the holocaust of the Second World War Shostakovich became convinced that mankind could not afford a third, and in March 1949 he headed a delegation to the Cultural and Scientific Conference for World Peace in New York. The delegation was welcomed and well received, but political pressures in the country curtailed the Russians' visit. In 1950 Shostakovich participated in the Second World Peace Congress at Warsaw; in 1952 he was a delegate at the World Peace Congress in Vienna; in 1954 he was awarded the Lenin Peace Prize.

The Tenth Symphony did not appear until 1953. It was premiered after Stalin's death and was a great success. Soviet realism it was not; instead, it was a deeply introspective work, as if the pain of the past five years was carefully expressed and analysed. Boris Schwarz said the score "heralded the liberalization of the human spirit." Shostakovich may not have held the score back any longer had Stalin remained alive, but with the man's death the mood in Russia melted into tolerance.* Shostakovich the artist had again timed it well, and the Tenth quickly became recognised as one of his masterpieces.

The Eleventh Symphony followed a busy four years. He released the Violin Concerto under a new opus number, 99 (old 77), in 1956 and his Second Piano Concerto in 1957. In 1954 his wife Nina died, and his mother passed away in 1955; Shostakovich re-married in 1956, to Margarita Andreyevna Kaymova. Never fond of travelling, Shostakovich guarded his privacy and became more and more of a recluse. Trips abroad were infrequent though requests were many; those he did make were usually in connection with peace conferences. His main activities remained teaching, rehearsals and composing.

In 1957 he finished his Eleventh Symphony, written to help commemorate the Fortieth Anniversary of the Revolution. The score was premiered in Moscow on October 30, 1957. Mravinsky conducted the Leningrad *première* on November 3. The symphony was an immediate and widespread success in Russia, equal in impact to the Fifth and

---

* Ironically, Sergey Prokofiev never had the chance to witness the thaw. He died the same day as Stalin, within hours of him, on March 5, 1953.

Seventh, and it earned its composer the Lenin Prize (old Stalin Prize) on April 28, 1958. In one move Shostakovich gave the Soviet leaders the heroic symphony they had always wanted, but gave it on his own terms.

In 1957 Shostakovich also spoke up for a free exchange between liberals such as himself and the conservationists who denigrated all Western influence in music as formalistic poison. That two factions existed at all was a definite improvement over 1948, when the First Composers' Congress was held. Now, at the Second Composers' Congress, Shostakovich, liberal in viewpoint though conservative in taste, acted as a bridge between the two sides. The government was another matter. During the Krushchev era the atmosphere relaxed, and Shostakovich took note of that at the Kremlin during a reception given for the Soviet intelligentsia on February 8, 1958. The dean of Russian composers expressed gratitude for the opportunities for artistic development that the Soviet state, as patron, offered its artists. This dual move by the political and artistic leaders lent an air of reconciliation, and even co-operation, between artist and state. Shostakovich, attacked in 1936 and 1948, was the ideal spokesman for the artists: only months before-hand he had achieved the very ideal for which the Soviets had always cried. Three months after the reception came the new Central Committee Decree that cleared most of the composers attacked by Zhdanov in 1948.

*

The success of the Eleventh Symphony promoted a warm and permissive atmosphere for Shostakovich which was further enhanced in November when the composer was awarded the Sibelius Prize at the University of Helsinki. In 1959 he presented a Cello Concerto which won quick approval.

Tension at home was easing as Krushchev spearheaded a policy of *détente* with the West and Eisenhower (and later Kennedy) sought *détente* with Russia. In the autumn of 1959 Shostakovich headed the first Russian cultural exchange group* to America—a trip which turned out to be much more pleasant and relaxed than his first visit ten years before. However, American audiences were not overly impressed by most of the Russian music they heard; only works by Shostakovich

---

* In the spring of 1958 Roger Sessions, Peter Mennin, Roy Harris and Ulysses Kay had gone to the Soviet Union. Aaron Copland and Lukas Foss went in the spring of 1960. Shostakovich went in the autumn of 1959 along with Khrennjkov, Kabalevsky, Konstantin Dankevich, Fikret Amirov and musicologist Boris Yarustovsky. Many such exchanges on all levels of the arts and humanities, and between almost all the countries of Europe, followed. While Shostakovich was in the U.S. he went to hear jazz titan Cannonball Adderley, and silently nodded his appreciation.

himself sparked any interest. In 1960 Shostakovich visited Dresden. While there he sought information from survivors of the Dresden fire bombing that had taken place on February 13, 1945, and the experience and impressions prompted him to compose his Eighth String Quartet, using the chamber format to express the deep and terrible feelings generated by the Dresden tragedy fifteen years after the fact. He subtitled the score, "In Memory of the Nazi and War Victims."

In this period of thaw 1961 was a memorable year. Shostakovich released the quartet and for the first time allowed the performance of his Fourth Symphony, which was well received in the U.S.S.R. and hailed abroad. At the same time Shostakovich planned to re-release *Lady Macbeth of Mtsensk* under the new title *Katerina Izmaylova*, with some minor alterations. What changes were made only served to improve the opera, which was also enthusiastically received. In 1961 Shostakovich also premiered his Twelfth Symphony and began working on a Thirteenth of daring proportions.

A young poet named Yevgyeni Yevtushenko had been writing poetry on controversial themes since his career began. His work both praised his homeland and talked in truthful terms of some of the uglier aspects of the country.* Yevtushenko was watched closely by more conservative writers and by his government. The poet's daring undoubtedly reminded Shostakovich of his own and the two combined forces to produce a symphony with chorus using the texts of five of Yevtushenko's poems. Even before the *première* of the symphony the cultural world in the Soviet Union buzzed with anticipation. The focal point for controversy was the first movement, using the words from a poem entitled "Babi Yar" which flashed back to an incident during World War Two when thousands of Jews and other Russians were butchered by the Nazi forces in a single sweep. The accusing poetic finger pointed to all anti-Semites—and to the Soviet government for not being against anti-Semitism and therefore being anti-Semitic itself. The idea behind the poem reached for the ideal behind Communism, that in order to work Communism must apply to every man. The Soviet government was not ready to adhere to or even allow that sentiment. Shostakovich obviously felt that it should be allowed—and vehemently expressed. Objections were levelled not against the music but against the content, and not just at "Babi Yar" but at all five poems.

The *première* of the symphony was anxiously awaited. The public was well aware of the pressure brought against the two artists and Krushchev himself strongly suggested at a meeting between the Soviet

---

* Yevtushenko, himself only twenty-nine in 1962, apparently captured the imagination of the new generation. Today he is a celebrity. His appeal among the young gave the Soviet government some concern but at the same time made him a strong bridge to youth for those in power.

Presidium and several hundred intellectuals, *avant-garde* artists and writers that the *première* be shelved. The suggestion was rejected. Rumours of cancellation abounded. People flocked to the *première* to see what the excitement was about, hoping not to be disappointed. The Conservatory Hall in Moscow was overflowing on the evening of December 18, 1962.

Boris Schwarz gave this account: ". . . The first half, consisting of Mozart's *Jupiter* Symphony, received a minimum of attention; no one cared . . . The intermission seemed endless; finally, the chorus filed on stage, followed by the orchestra, the soloist, the conductor Kirill Kondrashin. The tension was unbearable. The first movement, *Babi Yar*, was greeted with a burst of spontaneous applause. At the end of the hour-long work there was an ovation rarely witnessed. On the stage was Shostakovich, shy and awkward, bowing stiffly. He was joined by Yevtushenko, moving with the ease of a born actor. Two great artists —a generation apart—fighting for the same cause—freedom of the human spirit. Seeing the pair together, the audience went wild; the rhythmic clapping, so characteristic of Russian enthusiasm, redoubled in intensity, the cadence shouts 'Bra-vo Shos-ta-ko-vich' and 'Bra-vo Yev-tu-shen-ko' filled the air. The audience seemed to be carried away as much by the music as by the words, although (contrary to custom) the texts were not printed in the programme distributed to the public." ("Music and Musical Life in Soviet Russia"; London, 1972; p. 244.)

The next morning, however, there was no review in "Pravda," only a one-sentence announcement that the *première* had taken place.* Soon after that the second performance was postponed, due to the illness of a soloist. The Soviet leaders wanted Yevtushenko to make a few line changes in the *Babi Yar* movement, specifically to add words to indicate that not only Jews died there but also other Russians. It was further suggested that he add lines to show that the Russian people fought the Nazi menace with unity and purposefulness.† Yevtushenko made the

---

* Schwarz (*op. cit.*, pp. 367–8) gave this account: "The following morning, a one-sentence report appeared in *Pravda*, an absurd anti-climax for anyone who had witnessed the exciting evening. I rushed to the headquarters of the Composers' Union in search of a score or a piano reduction; I wanted to re-read the texts and evaluate their relationship to the music. My request was met with polite head-shaking and evasive excuses—the 'only' available score was in the hands of a critic who had failed to return it. . . . Needless to say, it was never returned, and all my efforts to have a glimpse of the score remained fruitless. Only later did I realize . . . there was an 'embargo' on the score because of official dissatisfaction with certain sections of the work. . . . This seemed patently absurd: the poem (Babi Yar) had been printed, recited, and televised around the world since 1961, and the delayed censorship was as pointless as it was idiotic."

† Anatoli Kuznetsov, who wrote a novel called "Babi Yar: A Document in the Form of a Novel," met with similar suggested censorship. The book as it was printed in Russia was void of any suggestion of Soviet wrong-doing at any time during the

alterations, but the four lines altered or added made no change on the overall impact. The new version was played on February 10, 1963. It was not played again until November 20, 1965, and then was dropped from the concert repertoire. The score appeared outside Russia only on January 17, 1970, when Eugene Ormandy conducted the Philadelphia Orchestra in its Western *première*. The version played was the *original* version, published by Leeds Music Publishers of Canada, and was hailed. Today the symphony is again played in Russia: through patience Shostakovich won another victory. Neither his nor Yevtushenko's stature suffered for the Thirteenth.

Why were the authorities so sensitive and critical so quickly? There was a power shake-up going on in the Presidium: Krushchev had barely contained the Cuban Missile Crisis, and as his solution was not satisfactory to many of his more militant compatriots a conservative, reactionary political tide was dawning and Krushchev's own political end was at hand. Against this backdrop Shostakovich continued to work for liberalisation. The period between the Thirteenth and Fourteenth Symphonies lasted seven years. Shostakovich began work on an opera, *And Quiet Flows the Don (Tikhi Don)*, but the work never appeared in his lifetime. In 1964 he collaborated with Yevtushenko again, this time to create a cantata based on a poem out of *Bratsk Station*, an epic series in praise of Russia's heritage and development. The poem-cantata, *The Execution of Stepan Razin (Kazn Stepana Razina)*, was a *tour de force* presentation of a heroic and romantic image. With it Shostakovich created a perfect example of programme music and also revealed his mystical side. Both artists had demonstrated that their former protest had come from a love that could now produce praise.

Meanwhile Shostakovich continued to drive himself. Teaching duties, composing and rehearsals kept him busy: he often attended rehearsals of many of his works to help performers with technical or interpretative difficulties. At home he and his wife enjoyed a quiet and carefully guarded solitude. In May 1966 Shostakovich did something he had not done in eight years: he gave a piano recital. Always trying to reach a personal rapport with his audience, he thoroughly enjoyed the experience, and the audience loved it, but the excitement of being on stage must have been too much. The day after the recital he suffered a major heart attack. He was fifty-nine.

He rebounded quickly and by September 25 of the same year he had recovered sufficiently to be permitted to travel to Leningrad to attend a concert given to honour him on his sixtieth birthday. His appearance was greeted with a standing ovation, and at the concert his Second Cello

---

period Kuznetsov discussed. When he defected to the West in 1969 he brought with him not only the original manuscript on microfilm, but also the information that pressure applied to artists in Russia remained extensive, in fact stifling.

Concerto was premiered. Shostakovich was also awarded the highest honour of the U.S.S.R., the first musician to be honoured as "Hero of Socialist Labour." At sixty he had become the spokesman for music in Russia and felt more and more ready to comment on its behalf. Shostakovich pushed hard to have new works by new composers premiered even when their compositions might have been a little too experimental for his personal taste. On May 18, 1968, in an interview with the monthly magazine "Yunost" (Youth), he explained his viewpoint on experimentalism: ". . . everything is good in moderation . . . The use of elements from these complex systems is entirely justified if it is dictated by the idea of the composition. . . Please understand that the formula 'the end justifies the means' to some extent seems right to me in music. And means? Any, as long as they convey the goal."

Shostakovich was soon back at work, presenting his Second Violin Concerto in June 1967. Then, as if to bolster his own viewpoint, two years after the concerto he produced the Fourteenth Symphony, totally apart from any other work he had ever created, yet perhaps the closest thing to a definitive demonstration of his musical and philosophical language. He had almost died in 1966; his heart never fully recovered from the strain. The immediacy of death now prompted him to depict what he saw and felt. Of all his works the Fourteenth was the most profound and will probably be considered the most significant and lasting. The very nature of the work, eleven poems set to chamber orchestra with a large complement of percussion and two solo voices, invited younger composers to follow suit and present equally imaginative and complex scores. During all the controls imposed on him in the past and all the periods of thaw that encouraged his voice, Shostakovich had strived for balance. Now he declared what that balance was. He still did not want the Russian artist or individual to forget his heritage or fail to draw from that heritage. As if to illustrate the point, he immediately followed the Fourteenth Symphony with a song-cycle built on pro-Lenin, pro-Revolution poetry by Yevgyeni Dolmatovsky. *Faithfulness*, for male chorus, was written to commemorate the hundredth anniversary of Lenin's birth. The standard, celebrant work appeared in 1970. Shostakovich was as sincere with this composition as with the symphony which preceded it.

At the age of sixty-five Shostakovich composed his Fifteenth Symphony over an eight-week period. As was his habit he kept the contents of the score a secret from family and friends until it was completed. Once he had it finished he showed it to his son, Maxim, who would conduct the world *première*. Two of Shostakovich's friends, composers Moysey Vaynberg and Boris Tchaikovsky, played the score on the piano for a small gathering: the response was favourable. Plans were made for the *première* in October, but Shostakovich grew ill and it was postponed.

The postponement served to increase the public's excitement and anticipation, always high for a Shostakovich *première* and compounded by the fact that Shostakovich's own son would conduct the piece (the first time for a major work). The *première* took place on January 8, 1972, in the Bolshoy Auditorium of the Moscow Conservatory, to a packed house with hopefuls standing in line waiting for cancellations. The performance was a triumph, and to a standing ovation the composer appeared on stage and kissed the conductor, his son.

No symphony followed the Fifteenth. Shostakovich composed only a few more works, among them his Fourteenth and Fifteenth Quartets. Like Beethoven, Shostakovich gave vent to his feelings in the chamber form at the end of his life. Even the Fifteenth Symphony had a chamber-like quality to its orchestration. Whereas Shostakovich had dedicated each of his Eleventh to Fourteenth Quartets to a member of the Borodin Quartet, his last one had no dedication—he was communing with himself. All his major works, from the 1966 heart attack onwards, held a certain intimacy.

On August 9, 1975, Shostakovich died of a heart attack at seven in the evening, Moscow time. Thousands filed past the open coffin, as he lay in state, to say goodbye.

First Symphony (1925)

The First Symphony is striking, and the versatility of the nineteen-year-old composer can immediately be appreciated by the listener. It is economically scored, with signs of both maturity and self-confidence. Shostakovich seems to be aware of his limitations, however, and endeavours to work within them: his use of piano in the second and fourth movements shows that, even though the composer is still a student of orchestration, he is very comfortable within his own limits, wisely relying on what he knows best.

The score draws for its stylistic language on several of Shostakovich's predecessors, particularly on Tchaikovsky with its lyricism and dancing nature; but the music shows also the sterner influence of Prokofiev, and especially of the *Scythian Suite* of 1914. Yet the sound already bears the unmistakable mark of what has come to be recognised as the true Shostakovich style, his orchestral ideas and his flair, even if the Mahlerian concept of the symphony as a grand, all-embracing work is yet to appear. The economy of orchestration does not detract from the power of the score; by contrast, both the Third and Fourth Symphonies, composed during a period of self-doubt and challenge to his musical beliefs, are over-orchestrated but are no more powerful in effect. In the First Symphony the composer seems to have no technical doubts and certainly displays none. He uses his resources to their fullest extent, electing to rely on the value and balance of his material to win audience approval instead of on the volume and dynamism of his orchestral writing. That his approach was absolutely right was proved by the enthusiastic praise showered upon the work by Glazunov and others when it was submitted as the thesis for his final examination at the Leningrad Conservatory in 1925. Its first public performance took place under Nikolay Malko on May 12 of the following year, winning for its author almost instant recognition as a major new voice in Russian music.

The symphony is in four movements played without a pause. The opening Allegretto is a comic Disneyesque dialogue between solo trumpet and bassoon, soon seized by clarinet as the celli run straight into a cul-de-sac. A momentary pause before the clowning continues—quietly but always with a threat of musical anarchy. A tiny taunting bassoon figure brings about the grotesque little tune for solo clarinet that is, in fact, the first subject of the Allegro Non Troppo:

Strings give this subject support and other instruments take up the catchy triplet fragment like members of an audience delightedly repeating a comedian's catch-phrase. Flute and bassoon take over the story but trumpet, apparently bored by the proceedings or simply jealous that its own phrase with which it opened the work has not met with such success, repeats it aggressively, and the music is thrown into momentary disarray.

A new departure is required, and is duly supplied by a solo flute with a pleasant waltz melody, taken perhaps as an act of compassion from the trumpet's phrase. The chamber textures are notable: rarely at this stage is Shostakovich willing to put the full weight of the orchestra to the test. At one point, built into the texture, the trumpet, *pp* and *espressivo*, nods as if in gratitude (or is it self-satisfaction?) that his phrase has at last been given due emphasis:

The waltz soon runs its inoffensive course and ceases, leaving a tenuous strand of sound that drifts into an ascending chromatic figure (two solo violins) that has already been heard in the introduction. Shostakovich is feeling his way carefully into a development section, allowing his listeners time to assimilate the somewhat fragmentary exposition and to realise that a new departure is about to take place. The two violins gruffly indicate their impatience; then abruptly the development is launched with growing vehemence and percussive insistence that rapidly threatens to get out of hand. Apologetically the music slips back into the brightness of F major and the simplicity of the 3/4 pulse as flute again presents its coy waltz. F minor and common time reappear and chaos threatens once more, brought about by the recapitulation of the clarinet's grotesque theme; but the fury quickly subsides in a bassoon solo that seems disillusioned with the triplet catch-phrase, and the clarinet recalls instead the introduction, now modified and shortened. The taunting bassoon figure that took us into the exposition is now transferred to celli to introduce the next movement.

In this Scherzo (allegro) the piano is heard for the first time, adding an unexpected incisiveness and brilliance to the sonorities. Low strings rush in, clarinet in its low register presents a loose, knockabout idea, and strings and horn scamper aimlessly until the piano, in a sudden downward glissando, pulls the threads together and the real business of the movement can be announced formally by violins. Almost before the Scherzo has started, however, it gives way to a cool Trio section of paired winds—flutes, then clarinets over a side-drum rhythm that imparts a funereal mood. Although this Trio is in duple time, the composer retains the 3/4 pulse, reinforcing the cross-rhythms by percussion and pizzicato strings. Through a gradual accelerando bassoon reintroduces the Scherzo and the music reaches a rushing climax, only to be severed by three sharp piano chords, fff. This rude interruption is so irrelevant to the progress of the music that the orchestra ceases to play, as if stunned. A broken attempt to restart is made by violas and celli, only to be crushed again by piano. In concert performance the final fff piano note, a low A for the pianist's right hand, presents a graphic image: the player crosses over to the bass of his instrument with a gesture oddly similar to the final, definitive, closing of the end cover of a large book. After this conclusive act of finality the music, unable to regain its breath, dies painfully. Up to this point the symphony has been basically optimistic in spirit, albeit unhealthily nervous, but by his unexpected and ruthless destruction of his Scherzo the young Shostakovich, personified in the piano part, shows unmistakably that he is already aware of violence and tragedy in music as well as in life. One wonders what his teachers at the Leningrad Conservatory made of this strange new voice, and how they imagined he could follow the savage act of vandalism wrought upon the Scherzo. It is unlikely that they would ever have guessed the course Shostakovich actually took.

Solo oboe announces the Lento in B flat minor over a shimmering string wash. The slow movement has brought a distinctly Tchaikovskian mood. Has Shostakovich destroyed his "modern" music only to return to the romantic notions of the previous century? Solo cello, that most melting and seductive of all orchestral voices, takes up the threnody; horns add pulsating harmonic richness, and, as in the opening movement of Tchaikovsky's First Piano Concerto (also in B flat minor), there is a distant quasi-military trumpet fanfare:

Passion and intensity increase with the dynamic level, and the fanfare, far from being a passing reference, rapidly assumes prime importance, passing from instrument to instrument as the music blackens. Solo oboe suggests another melody, this time with a hint of the dotted fanfare about it, and soon harsh brass chords bring a hardening of the texture. Eventually a solo violin introduces a moment of peace and stillness, only to be contradicted by the fanfare *motif*, pulling the music forcefully and repeatedly into passive acceptance of its unyielding rhythm. Muted trumpet, *pianissimo*, takes up the oboe's second melody as strings divide themselves into no fewer than sixteen voices, drawing a tenuous veil of sound over this profoundly troubled movement.

A side-drum roll swells from *pianissimo* to *forte*, startling the Finale into life. Two flutes and an oboe, soon joined by clarinet, alternate with low strings in an introductory Lento, to some extent and with evident difficulty clearing away the doubts of the slow movement to prepare for the main part of the Finale. The Allegro Molto is propelled forward by two clarinets and, as in the Scherzo, a piano is introduced to lend cohesion to music that threatens to fly apart under the force of its own velocity. At the height of the exposition violins and violas sing out a new and romantic melody with all possible strength:

The temperature drops sharply (*meno mosso*, crotchet=144) as a solo violin sings a lamenting second subject, the continuation of which is set under a wavering accompaniment as flutes tremble chromatically in an effect extraordinarily like the *timbre* of a musical saw. The development concentrates a great amount of material and activity into a small space, as if anxious to cover as much ground as possible before what is coming to be regarded as the inevitable collapse. Already our brief experience of Shostakovich the symphonist has led us to expect that when his music encompasses great stress and energy there must come a breaking point. When it comes in this Finale it is a stroke of such sublime simplicity that it carries the maximum power: the music reaches a shrill climax and stops abruptly as if it had become aware in a flash of an indescribably terrible element. The obsessive rhythm that had brought such pain in the slow movement is heard, inverted, *fff*, on solo timpani. Three times it challenges the Finale, gradually diminishing in power; such is its influence that the back of the movement is broken. Slowly, as if labouring under a great weight, a solo muted cello intones the great violin melody (see above example), but the ominous rhythm lingers like a spectre until the end of the movement, despite a valiant attempt by the strings to reintroduce their romantic melody in augmentation:

At the very end it is the military rhythm, slightly slurred in its heady victorious rush, that triumphs:

Second Symphony, "To October" (1927)

The Second, in one movement, is the shortest of all the symphonies, requiring barely nineteen minutes to perform. It is Shostakovich's first orchestral effort as a result of his post-graduate exposure to modern music, and in its orchestration succumbs to a popular fad of the day—factory music—including in the score a real factory whistle or hooter (a part which may be taken by brass if required*) as an allusion to the magnificent progress being made by Soviet factories in the task of building the new, post-Revolutionary nation. The concept of ultra-realism was not new in Russian music and it was only logical that the youthful composer should experiment, no matter how modestly. In none of his programmatic symphonic works did the composer bluntly state his programme—merely a concrete concept that the audience might use to relate to the abstract sphere of the music. Often he only supplied subtitles to his movements for this effect. The appearance of a factory hooter in the Second Symphony may add a touch of realism, but when orchestral brass are substituted the moment of industrial

---

* To date, all recordings have opted for the orchestral alternative.

realism can be missed unless the listener has the score to hand or is forewarned in some other way. The real message of the symphony is entrusted to the choir, as we shall see.

The symphony is dedicated to October 1917, the month and year of the Bolshevik Revolution. The composer employed revolutionary poetry as a basis for the choral ending, but in that peroration he does not tell a story *per se*: rather, he sings the praises of the Soviet state and its people, and tells of a hopeful future. The work may not be great, but it is important in the artist's development, and it has been largely ignored because it is not immediately accessible to listeners outside Russian culture and experience. Its programme and methods are dated and the poetry at the end of the work is specifically Soviet in content; for anyone outside Russia the score therefore appears foreign and propagandistic. Yet the work is an interesting statement by a young artist trying to make sense of a great event that changed his country just at the time he himself would have become politically aware. It shows Shostakovich's ability to relate the feelings of a nation through his own feelings.

The symphony opens mysteriously, on the threshold of hearing, as a web of sound on muted strings begins to grow. This effect is created in a notable way: an extended metrical accelerando built into a fixed tempo. Double basses begin on even crotchets in bar 2 over a faint cymbal and bass-drum roll, and in bar 5 violas begin a triplet quaver pattern. Bar 9 finds one group of second violins in semiquavers, while in bar 12 the other group of second violins continues the web with a mixture of straight and triplet semiquavers. Bar 12 is quoted here:

When one group of first violins enters it follows the semiquaver mixture of the second violins' top line, but when the last group—the rest of the first violins—finally completes the web in bar 20 it is moving in continuous semiquaver triplets. The accelerando is therefore achieved by progressive metrical diminution within an unchanging tempo and without any one group of instruments changing its basic rhythmic beat. This extraordinary passage, highly chromatic and with one 5/4 and one 7/4 bar inserted against the common-time signature, is continued unchanged and at *ppp* for thirty-six bars at *largo* tempo, an amazing and disturbing commencement to a symphony and one perhaps designed to give a feeling of instability, distant chaos, almost of blind wandering. Above this confusion of string voices enters a slowly evolving and mutating brass chord from which a trumpet solo emerges in ghostly fashion, aimlessly groping for a theme. Piccolo and flute in unison continue the search, and the further entry of horns and trumpets, still *pianissimo*, brings us to the point at which the string web finally disintegrates, leaving solo cello and two solo double basses muttering in triplet semiquavers. A solo tuba, *ppp*, joins the search for a theme but abandons it after a few minutes on a profoundly mystical low A flat as the *largo* tempo is at last relieved. A long, fantastic, prancing *fugato* brings an overdue sense of movement, if not direction. Crashing timpani, thrusting basses, and another tuba solo announce a new and disruptive section; eventually a solo violin leads a dance-like passage, quickly joined by clarinet and bassoon, then by the rest of the strings, oboes, flutes, and other instruments in ones and twos, until fifteen separate but inter-related paths form a frenetic *mêlée* of dense and excitable sound. Again it is the timpani that demand a change, this time to a stately horn melody which lasts but three bars yet acts as a steadying influence on the still volatile music. Ultimately a long clarinet solo, giving way to solo violin, leads gently into the first example of realism in the symphony: the factory hooter in F sharp, and the entrance of the chorus.

From this moment the music assumes a much more traditional style. Some critics feel that the choral ending was simply tacked on the score, not as a logical conclusion to the piece but merely for the sake of finding a stirring ending, and one that would put the composer into grace with his narrow-minded political bosses, regardless of the unity of the symphony. Nowhere is it recorded whether Shostakovich was in favour of or against the Communist principle: perhaps he was apolitical, content to acknowledge the Soviet ideal every so often in return for being allowed to compose what he felt urged to compose. It may be that the young composer fervently believed in Alexandr Bezimensky's revolutionary lines as he set them chorally to celebrate the tenth anniversary of the Revolution, but the fact remains that, with all its grand gestures and posturing, the last six minutes or so of the Second Symphony are very much less interesting than the first thirteen.

The factory hooter (or horns, trombones and trumpets in unison) introduces misery-laden verses describing the plight of ordinary workers

before the Revolution. In the distance a striving figure is heard on
trumpet—perhaps the beginning of hope for the oppressed people. The
chorus relates the destiny of Russia, to fight, and then the achievements of the Soviet state. The composer provides a strong and certain
orchestral background for the chorus. Gradually the mood brightens and
the striving figure, at its most imperious on solo horn,

gains in importance as the music builds to an extraordinary passage of
declamation: tenors, basses, tenors again, altos, then the whole chorus
shout: "Our banner! The name of our cause: October! Communism!
Lenin!" The orchestra then closes swiftly in triumphant air, with one of
Shostakovich's shortest codas.

Third Symphony, "May Day" (1929)

Like the Second Symphony, the Third is in one movement, but it is at once more elaborate and linear. The music is less abstract but is filled with fantastic ideas and effects that reveal Shostakovich yet again as a true craftsman. Some critics have stated, perhaps with justification, that the score is over-orchestrated, a sign of the composer's lack of confidence during this period, and we shall have occasion to point out the way in which his apparent mastery of the orchestral palette acts against musical effect. The Third is grandiose in scope, effect and performance and is a veritable well of themes and ideas, clearly demonstrating, in an orgy of creativity, the considerable extent of the composer's skills to date: an array of the extensive technical resources which were to be harnessed and brought to bear on his mature works. This is Shostakovich's most brilliantly optimistic symphony. Victor Seroff called it a "proletarian tract in tones," and its dazzling orchestration and abundantly joyous themes indeed make it a delightful study in humour and wit that may be appreciated by all classes of society. However, the score received a mixed reception. Together with the Second Symphony and his opera of the absurd, *The Nose*, the Third was seen uneasily as the continued development of a new *enfant terrible* in Russia. On the other hand, there was little basis for any hope that Shostakovich would become the new leader of radicalism in music. Even in the Third he shows his conservatism, experimenting and then retreating to allow more conventional sounds to make his point.

The Third Symphony, subtitled "May Day" or "First of May" (Pyervoye maya), premiered by the Leningrad Philharmonic Orchestra under Alexandr Gauk on January 21, 1930, is little known outside the Soviet Union, and even there it tends to be dismissed as an early effort; yet once again it is a vital work in our understanding of the composer's development. The music is strong and emotional, the work of a youth hard-pressed to surpass his First Symphony and endeavouring to establish a reputation among the new school of Soviet artists. Certain passages are immediately appealing, others less so in their unbridled fantasy, while amid the high-spirited writing drama abounds. The four divisions of this single movement fit, in condensed form, the same moods so prominent in the composer's four-movement format: doubt/dance/doubt/hope.

At the very start the solo clarinet, *allegretto*, sets a mood of fantasy in an oddly-shaped theme that tries to be pensive but succeeds in being merely bizarre:

Celli and basses *pizzicato* sketch in a rhythm, another clarinet joins the first, and the music grows in stature and beauty. Solo trumpet proposes a new idea, answered at length by woodwind as a solo horn adds further commentary in similar style, but discussion is curtailed by a sudden crescendo into the Allegro, pieces of melody being scattered like confetti in a gust of wind. A strongly syncopated viola and cello melody is taken up half-heartedly by the solo trumpet and then submerged in a wealth of melodic and rhythmic ideas before a brass march enters, complete with its own touch of syncopation. But the music is too impatient for anything so staid as a march, even a rakishly syncopated one, and this in turn is swallowed up in the flying music. Shostakovich's ability to write music of unremitting impetus is shown many times in the first four symphonies and it was to bring immense rewards in the Tenth and Eleventh after he had brought self-discipline to bear on his material.

At last the music reaches, via a plummeting figure on wind and strings, a slower section with a prominent viola and clarinet ostinato used as a darkening device to accompany another fantastic melody, this one announced by violins. The slower tempo is clearly displeasing to the coarser members of the brass family, who jeer rudely and are plainly delighted when the strings abandon their idea and bring the tempo up again to its previous level. In fact, while the rest of the orchestra whirls somewhat ineffectually, it is the brass that carries the thematic weight of this part of the work. Here is the evidence to support those critics who point to Shostakovich's early orchestration as immature : his scoring is so very thick and eventful that only the strident melody-carriers of the brass department can hope to cut through it. Consequently, horn, trombone, and particularly trumpet, take the lion's share of thematic responsibility and, although the music has infinite panache, it is ultimately somewhat restricted in tonal variety for all its endlessly varied scoring.

An abrupt stop brings a side-drum solo as an accompaniment for a melody, in almost pioneering spirit, for two horns in unison :

Trumpet joins in, and as the percussion ceases a brilliantly humorous episode for woodwind with prominent piccolo allows many instrumentalists to display their remarkable agility, even including the timpanist, as spirits descend for the introduction of the *andante* section. Violins, *ppp* in their upper register, announce a grotesque theme, only to be interrupted by timpani and brass in disruptive mood. Despite the mainly slow tempo and low dynamic level, this section, corresponding to a slow movement, is eventful as well as being highly charged with emotion. Several times the melody tries to grow and develop but the all-enveloping nervousness never allows this to happen. Giving up the effort, the music breaks again into *allegro* tempo, running breathlessly with an even quaver rhythm, instruments dancing over a backdrop of strings in a manner later identifiable in any Shostakovich scherzo:

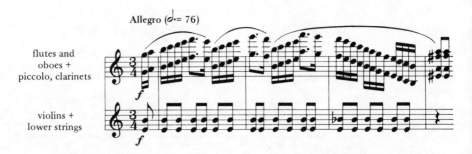

Brass once again climb to the forefront, the rhythm changes to a gallop, then back to a canter, and finally to a more dignified pace as strings and wind play a noble theme against constant interruptions from impatient brass. At last the bottled-up nervousness is released in a huge climax as a strange unison arches and writhes over a deadening roar of percussion, bass drum repeatedly sealing the fate of the slowly dissolving statement until only a valiant tuba is left.

In an exploratory section of ominous bass *glissandi* and a powerfully orating trombone, the music seeks a new level of consciousness.

It finds it in a Moderato in which a string unison under wind chords introduces the choral section. This is full-throated, melodic, attractive, and composed in a style designed to be easily assimilated and remembered; as in the Second Symphony the message is idealogical, the words by S. Kirsanov telling of the new horizons of Communism, and of the First of May throwing its light into the eyes of the future. The final bars feature a thrilling trumpet solo reaching ever and again to a brilliant and piercing clarino top B flat.

The Third Symphony is a remarkable achievement by a twenty-three-year-old composer under the pressures of success that Shostakovich faced. The boldness of the score may hide the shyness of the composer but in it he develops a unifying rhythmic "signature": one long beat followed by two short ones. He also better solved the problem of a choral ending than in the Second, but curiously did not attempt another choral symphony until 1962: although he intended to include choral sections in his Sixth, Seventh and Ninth Symphonies, it was not until the Thirteenth that voices again found a place in his expressive needs on a symphonic level. Meanwhile, the Third stands as a flawed, over-scored, but fascinating and thoroughly enjoyable work with a melodic content so rich and varied as to border on the wasteful. Shostakovich's teeming imagination was slow to learn economy.

Fourth Symphony (1935/36)

With the two symphonies of the late twenties Shostakovich tried to keep the programme proletarian while making the music progressive. His youthfulness, the nature of his government, his position as a closely-watched musical celebrity, his personal pressures and his own artistic needs undermined these attempts and their reception by others. It seems that about this time he was anxious to establish his own musical individuality and the Fourth Symphony was the culmination of his experimentation and self-identification. It has no programme whatever, no words to hint at its meaning. It is absolute music in the purest sense, exploring further towards horizons that were now discouraged or even banned outright from 1932 onwards.

For a long time the Fourth was a missing link between the odd-sounding and grandiose early symphonies and the apparently about-face Fifth. When Shostakovich came under attack in 1936 he withdrew the score at its tenth rehearsal and did not allow the *première* to take place until almost nine years after Stalin's death. Those who saw the score at the time of its shelving noticed a simple remark on it: "Withdrawn." For twenty-five years the composer kept it sequestered. In 1946 a lithographed version for two pianos appeared but this led to no great stirring of interest in the work. After Stalin's death Shostakovich could have had the score premiered at any time, but he withheld it until December 30, 1961. It appeared in the West shortly thereafter.*

It is generally granted that Shostakovich withdrew the Fourth Symphony because he was afraid of the response it would receive after the 1936 attack on him. However, this is evidently not the whole story. He recognised that the work had its weaknesses, as he wrote in 1956: "Also a failure was my Fourth Symphony, not played as yet. It is—as far as form is concerned—a very imperfect, long-winded work that suffers—I'd say—from 'grandiosomania.' However, the score contains some parts I like." Presumably it was for these "some parts" that Shostakovich at last allowed the *première* to go ahead, as well as to satisfy the curiosity of others.

The symphony, although generally considered not to be amongst his best works, has won praise and universal admiration as one of his most original and interesting scores. Despite a certain dependence on other symphonists (in addition to Mahler as discussed below, the Nielsen of the Sixth Symphony will occasionally enter the mind of the listener) it is distinctly experimental and rich in ideas. Many see it as representative of the direction Shostakovich's language would have followed had he been free to develop (whether inside Russia or out) but this is a slanted viewpoint. The Fourth points a straight line between the Third and Fifth Symphonies, being an extension of the experimental ideas of the Second and Third which Shostakovich also considered to be "failures." Still searching for an identity, the composer produced a radical new work that expanded on everything he had learned so far. The key to the work is its use of free form; and it is perhaps an indication of what happens when the composer lets his ideas flow freely without a precise structure. Had the composer so wished, he could have reduced the criticism that his symphony was formless to nonsense, as did Satie who, when critics told him that his music was "shapeless," solemnly produced *Three Pieces in the Shape of a Pear (Trois morceaux en forme de poire)*. Shostakovich had only to explain that, far from being formless, his Fourth Symphony had a unique and totally individual form: that of Shostakovich's Fourth Symphony. What these critics should have had the perception to say was that the work does not fall neatly into their preconceived notions of the form a symphony should take. As far as we know, the composer did not issue a statement in defence of his music, and, with the exception of only one or two commentators and a handful of conductors, the musical world does not

---

* The first Western recording, by Eugene Ormandy and the Philadelphia Orchestra, was issued in 1962.

seem to have had much knowledge of it. It is time more words were said in favour of the work. First of all, it should be pointed out that there never has been a fixed rule demanding that the first movement of a symphony, or any other movement for that matter, must be in sonata form, or rondo, or variation form, or whatever. A number of utterly convincing symphonic movements exist that have little or nothing to do with established forms, breaking new formal paths without destroying either existing patterns or their composers' reputations. Secondly, if Shostakovich's Fourth does not replace time-honoured forms with cogent, memorable and easily assimilable alternatives, it is still far from "formless" and contains much fine music, and it is up to us to shelve our preconceptions in order to enjoy that music. It is easy to see what it was in the music that the composer liked. Doubtless he was referring to some of the delicious scoring and melodic ideas that, in another sphere, might make brightly successful ballet music. Thirdly, the episodic nature of the construction brings with it an intellectual freedom which allows the listener to enjoy the many aural extravagances of the score without feeling uneasy that an important structural point has been missed, or a vital thematic reference overlooked. It should be made clear that the Fourth and Fifth Symphonies are totally independent works: in withdrawing the former under criticism and replying to that criticism with the latter Shostakovich did not simply take the material of the Fourth and remould it. Even if that had been possible it is unlikely that such a fluent composer would have found it necessary to resort to that kind of patching. On the other hand, certain elements clearly survived the self-critical (or self-preserving) crisis surrounding the withdrawal of the Fourth and turn up again in the Fifth. They are surprisingly few in number and are almost unimportant enough to be described as inadvertent similarities of the sort one finds in the music of most composers.

We have, then, two entirely independent symphonies: the Fourth brings to an end the composer's youthful period while the Fifth begins his mature one.

It was suggested above that the aural delights of the Fourth Symphony may be appreciated without necessarily relating them to other events, either musical or extra-musical. The commentary that follows, therefore, makes no attempt to discuss the music symphonically in the way that has been attempted in other works.* Instead, remarks are made upon events as they follow each other in the hope that the

* Both Ormandy and Kondrashin demonstrate in their recordings how difficult it is to prevent the score from rambling. Kondrashin manages this feat more successfully, but the Philadelphia Orchestra under Ormandy plays with great force and distinction. Previn, on the other hand, tends to play down the fantastic element; in some ways his reading is the most "symphonic" of all.

listener will appreciate for their own sake the often extraordinary ideas without being disorientated by their apparent lack of growth and continuity. Labels such as "exposition," "development," etc., being irrelevant, have been avoided as much as possible.

From the first moment one is reminded of Mahler's bizarre orchestration and grotesque melodies. Three screaming chords, each prefaced by discordant grace-notes, bring a gawky idea on higher woodwind, *marcatissimo* and *ff*, supported by xylophone. This in turn brings a stamping rhythm over which two trombones and two trumpets present a theme clearly related, as a black sheep may be to the rest of the flock, to the main theme of the Finale of the Fifth Symphony (see example on page 71).

The stamping gradually exhausts itself to give way to a *legato* string idea notable for its fidgety changes of metre, but edges soon recur and the music builds back to the stamping, if not to the theme, of the opening section. Bleak woodwind triplets interrupted by *pizzicato* chords

develop into a twisted woodwind unison cut off peremptorily by solo timpani. By now, some six minutes into the movement and with hardly an idea repeated (apart from a rhythmic horn *motif*) it is to be expected that the "exposition" section should end and some of the wealth of material thus exposed be "developed." The Fourth is, however, no ordinary symphony and it is evident that the composer's vast fund of melodic, rhythmic and colouristic ideas is by no means exhausted. Low strings, then woodwind, toy with the timpani rhythm, putting it to playful use and then, unaccountably, an expressive melody on celli and basses brings a moment of naked wrath. A pensive bassoon plaint initiates a section in which the music pauses as if in quiet agitation, the opening paragraph of the symphony suggested vaguely by thematic and rhythmic fragments. The internal stress of the music increases and brass join battle as vicious jagged fragments are thrown from instrument to instrument and the music fills with pain until, without warning, the first theme trots in on piccolo and the little E flat clarinet, as if happy to be back and innocently unaware of what has been taking place. Woodwind hold the stage for a time but are increasingly challenged, first by brass, then by *pizzicato* strings, in spite of which they maintain the lighter mood, eventually giving way to an extraordinarily strenuous string fugue built on a fiercely buzzing subject:

In performance the section quoted above takes approximately four seconds to play, so precipitate is the music. For 137 bars the fugue hurtles along, catching other instruments in its slipstream and finally, perhaps inevitably, falling on *fortissimo* percussion in a passage which may have been resurrected for use in the Finale of the Fifth Symphony at the point which leads into the development. Timpani, woodblock, side drum and bass drum pound out a frenetic unison over which the whole brass section tries to re-establish the opening subject, only to find, when the shouting dies, that a broken, grimacing version of it survives aggressively on strings, suddenly to be transformed into a leering waltz garnished with the minatory tone of bass clarinet. The waltz is taken up joyfully by lower strings under curious fluttering high woodwind chords before it disintegrates, disappearing in a descending *glissando* like water down a basin outlet. A series of juddering chords follows, building from *pp* to *fffff* and from the confusion is torn what sounds like a recapitulation of the opening theme, but the music side-steps as two trumpets and two muted trombones put forward an oddly transformed version of it in 6/8 time. Solos on cor anglais, solo violin (a particularly beautiful one in a movement all too lacking in beauty) and bassoon (a very quiet, faithful and extended restatement of the first theme) gradually allow the movement to sink to rest.

The second movement, *moderato con moto*, is the most conventional of the three, being in a regular 3/8 pulse, based on D, and developing only two main themes. The first part, that which would be termed "scherzo" in a more commonly-conceived symphony, is presented in rich string tones

then taken through its paces, variously employing all the instruments. Notable once again are two of Shostakovich's favourites: the piccolo clarinet in E flat and the bass clarinet in B flat, the one hectic and pure-toned, the other almost unbelievably sinister. Both appear frequently in the symphonies, but in the case of the bass clarinet it is not until the Finale of the Eleventh Symphony that its amazingly menacing character is used to maximum advantage, as we shall see. A Trio section,

more stately in nature and clearly an ancestor of the first theme of the opening movement of the Fifth Symphony (see example on page 67), enters on violins and develops more freely over a low string backdrop, the development growing in strength until contradicted by timpani chords. An extended *fugato* on the scherzo theme follows before the Trio returns on four horns, the accompanying rhythmic *motif* previously entrusted to violas now on all the woodwind except the small clarinet. The traditional Beethoven scherzo/trio pattern of ABABA is now completed by the final appearance of the opening theme on muted violin demisemiquavers over *pizzicato* bass and a tolling low D on harp, but it is the extraordinarily captivating percussion accompaniment that will most readily catch the ear:

If references to Mahlerian style were to be found in the opening and the bird-like woodwind calls of the first movement, Shostakovich's debt to the Austrian composer becomes even more obvious at the start of the Finale: over solemn timpani and double bass crotchets the solo bassoon announces a funeral march, a sombre and beautiful theme promising a fascinating movement.*

* Ormandy is particularly brilliant here, an excellence not altogether maintained later in the movement.

Bass clarinet and double bassoon add their ponderous voices, and an oboe extends the idea. Various woodwind instruments carry or embellish the funeral *motif* through several variations, trumpets and horns taking it up over string semiquavers as the music moves into a new episode announced by violins over continuing semiquavers. The funeral march returns—or reasserts itself, for it seems hardly to have been absent. Insistence on a high G (oboes, clarinets, flutes and piccolo) over angrily thrusting low strings forms a short and dramatic bridge to the *allegro* section, commencing like an ungainly dance but evidently with ample reserves of power and energy. The episode resembles the pre-choral part of the Third Symphony. Momentum increases as much use is made of a simple but effective rhythmic device divided between high and low voices, extending, while mutating harmonically, for thirty bars:

This scherzo-like but earnest passage gathers instruments in increasing numbers and intensifies in fury, only to reach, not the expected climax, but a sudden collapse on low horn pedals, only to give way to a whimsical theme on bass clarinet interrupted by piccolo, a theme which turns out to be nothing more than an introduction to an ingratiating waltz in which muted celli, then woodwind and violins, in a prime example of delicate scoring, take the mood gently from Viennese grace, yet again strongly recalling Mahler, to a humorous, almost vaudevillian, breathlessness. The combinations are wild, almost anarchic, and a trombone solo, in trying to bring order to the disintegrating music, merely succeeds in compounding the confusion. It is left to another waltz, of which Shostakovich has a seemingly endless fund, to restore order, even the trombone at last conforming, to the best of its coarse-grained ability, to the decorous mood. A change to 2/4 time brings a hurried passage for strings alone, again interrupted by trombone, but the urgency in the music cools as a magical section of gently glowing upper string harmonies over pattering celli and basses seems to move the listener to an ethereal plane of rarefied delight. The symphony is clearly drawing to a close, its troubles resolved, its message of hope and happiness brought home with utmost lucidity to reassure a confused and puzzled listener. Basses peter out as the violins and violas fade to nothing in a clear, cloudless sky of utter peace; then Shostakovich springs one of his most ruthless and dramatic strokes. Two timpani, later strengthened by string basses *ff*, hammer out an awkward canonic figure in a savage ostinato as the brass hurls out a series of harsh chords striving upwards, then downwards, in a mighty climax which recalls the funeral march amid a volcanic, all-obliterating blare of sound. But at once it is over; and softly, in a concluding valediction as different in tone from that heartless onslaught as that was from the preceding episode, the Fourth Symphony melts away in a remarkable coda. Celesta sounds a nine-note phrase

celesta
(over spread
C major
string chord)

repeated three more times before giving way to a soulful muted trumpet. Further reiterations of the celesta figure, the last extended by two notes, leave an unresolved ending over a bare C major chord, as if that last monstrous interruption had shattered all hope of a solution to the problems posed by the symphony.

Fifth Symphony (1937)

With this work Shostakovich scored a triumph that brought him lasting fame. It is interesting that the score achieved success despite its being contrary in mood and style to what the Soviet authorities required from a symphony. In 1937 they did not want tragedy in art, yet the Fifth is tragic. They did not want formalism, yet the score is abstract and formalistic, at least in its reliance on sonata form and other established practices, while still retaining a certain looseness within those precepts. The Soviet leaders wanted folk music and nationalistic ideas; the Fifth contains none. The second movement is a grotesque dance based upon themes from the still unperformed Fourth Symphony that had parodied the very critics who had ostracised the composer in 1936. Yet the score was such a massive *tour de force* that it melted away all opposition.

Shostakovich did not waver from his musical beliefs in this symphony despite its apparently yielding subtitle, "A Soviet Artist's Reply to Just Criticism." Instead, he resisted the pressures of 1936. It was as if he were providing his critics with an answer and then silently laughing at them. The only major difference from former works was the cohesiveness of the presentation. That was his true reply to what the composer saw as truly just criticism; Shostakovich looked inside himself, saw perhaps for the first time that some of the barrage of criticism he had encountered might be valid, and immediately withdrew the Fourth Symphony, labelling it later as a failure. For almost two years he separated the "worthless" from the just criticism, but by supplying such a submissive title he could allow the state to think that they were the critics he heeded. In Russia there is a saying for what he did: "Kiss, but spit."

The Fifth Symphony is heroic in nature, more so than any of its predecessors, but even though the heroic ideal had always been present in his symphonies, here for the first time it was expressed to satisfaction because it was expressed subjectively. The hero of this score is the composer himself. Bearing in mind all the uncertainties concerning acceptance, the past attacks, Shostakovich's self-doubts, and the nature of the score itself, it is amazing how restrained and balanced the work turned out to be. The only conclusion can be that Shostakovich believed so fervently in his score that he had no doubts about its value, only about its acceptance. The Fifth was a challenge rather than an apology, despite the way in which the state received it.

Its positive reception, however, was ecstasy for Shostakovich. So impressed was everyone with the work that several men who later chose to write biographies of the composer called the Fifth a turning point, a Rubicon. They had had no exposure to the linking Fourth Symphony, but even if they had they would hardly have recognised the link publicly. The Fifth was seen as a heroic work on heroic themes. Ivan Martinov thought it an autobiographical symphony depicting the hard road that the hero—Shostakovich himself—had travelled. Certainly it was a smoother and more accessible symphony than either the Second or the Third, its ideas presented more logically and linearly. In the Fifth the composer defined once and for all both his style and his art-form.

Shostakovich himself wrote: "The theme of my symphony is the making of a man. I saw man with all his experience in the centre of the composition, which is lyrical in form from beginning to end. The Finale is the optimistic solution of the tragically tense moments of the first movement." That was all the programme the artist himself supplied: the formulation of a personality.

The first movement, *moderato* leading to *allegro non troppo*, commences with a strenuous string figure in canon consisting initially of leaping and falling minor sixths quickly narrowing to thirds.

(see example at top of facing page)

A compromise is eventually established as lower strings mutter sequences of fourths, still in close canon, while the first violins quietly announce the opening subject. This is a beautiful, expansive theme, immediately possessed of the composer's penchant for tension and nervousness.

Above all, it is majestic and strong, as if rising above the subdued turmoil of its accompaniment, yet as this accompaniment abruptly ceases, the first subject succumbs to the opening leaping figure, immediately giving way altogether as two bassoons state their own version of it in portly octaves. The contenders in the music are thus introduced and have already displayed their differences of outlook: the one stern and uncompromising, the other yielding but, as we shall see, possessed of an inner resilience. First violins now develop the latter in a long *cantilena*, almost pleading at times, and with occasional support from two flutes. This passage is unexpectedly reminiscent of Berlioz in pastoral or nocturnal mood, yet there is little of Nineteenth-century romanticism in the music as it moves inevitably into harsh conflict, horns, then trumpets, taking up fragments from both sides without at this stage committing themselves totally to either. Abruptly a more delicate idea is announced, again on first violins, over a pulsating accompaniment of lower strings.

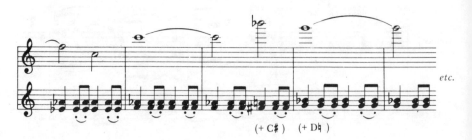

It is not immediately apparent that this lyrical melody, one of the most heartbreakingly lovely in Twentieth-century music, is none other than that first grotesque leaping figure magically transformed. The stress inherent in those minor sixths is replaced by consoling octaves, and the anger in the fierce dotted rhythm is smoothed away by the simple but effective method of enormous augmentation. The child-like innocence of this passage quickly evaporates, however, as warnings of conflict are heard again in the lower strings, then in stern but quiet chords from bass woodwind alternating with a heartfelt flute solo, soon taken up by clarinet. For a moment the lyrical melody returns but a descent through the strings brings the tragic kernel of the movement: over an agitated rhythm supported by piano, four horns pronounce the onset of the conflict as the two diverse elements struggle for supremacy in a passage that terrifyingly coalesces into a grim march.

As timpani and side drum cease their rhythm, woodwind and strings in tortured unisons, *fortissimo*, restate the leaping opening figure, and in a frenzy of tight canonic imitation the climax of the conflict is reached: a full-throated restatement of the violin's pleading *cantilena* on higher woodwind and strings, with horns, punctuated by timpani and brass chords, *largamente*, and culminating after ten bars in a *molto ritenuto*. Like a sorrowing procession, a linking passage, comprising the rhythmic tag from the accompaniment of the lyrical subject but now hammered out *con tutta forza*, together with echoes from the leaping *motif* (bassoons, low brass and low strings, *fortissimo*), leads to a wonderful restatement of the child-like subject on flute and horn in relaxed canon. Clarinet, with piccolo, and then with oboe and bassoon, extend this into a typically regretful Shostakovich leave-taking. Other instruments, notably solo violin and celesta, bring about a conclusion of unresolved doubt, elements of the disruptive leaping figure enduring to the end.

A comparison between this first movement and that of Nielsen's Fifth Symphony (1922) is unavoidable. The same spirit of warring musical elements is heard in both, as is the uneasy victory at the end, but the similarity will be observed most pointedly, if superficially, in the central sections where marching timpani crotchets and a repetitive side-drum rhythm impart to the music an unmistakably military mood. But Shostakovich's movement is no mere copy. One feels the music as a logical result of the composer's work up to that time, modified by official pressure indeed, and also tamed by what appears to be a newly-found desire in the composer to be more accessible. Whether or not the Russian knew the music of his Danish contemporary, hindsight tells us that Shostakovich's development was ready for this closely-reasoned first movement; and even if the musical elements had been totally different a similarly powerful and stressful movement would have resulted.

If Nielsen provided some of the inspiration for the first movement, it is to Mahler's wry humour that Shostakovich turned in his "Scherzo." This Allegretto is a witty, biting satire of barely four minutes' duration, and gives intellectual relief from the concentration of the first movement. Quickly, loudly, moving at a pace that seems to tax them, the low strings introduce the dance

and then woodwinds talk in orderly fashion.

The horns play their own march-like theme, and each section takes its turn with its identifying theme. The movement is gay, raucous, but at the same time nervous, its energies playfully expended to provide a moment of comic relief heightened by the judicious insertion of an occasional common-time bar within the basic 3/4 pulse. Formally, the movement is in the expected ABA scherzo pattern, the central B (trio) section well-integrated into the music as a solo violin presents its own version, almost an *inversion*, of the orderly woodwind passage, replacing their trills with *glissandi* which often lead to a harmonic on top E. The *glissando* idea is taken up by other instruments, none more successfully than the harp, as flute holds the melody, before the main part of the Scherzo returns in greatly modified form. Now, bassoon and double bassoon take the weight of the gawky first subject, and much of the ensuing restatement is played *pizzicato* at a low dynamic level. Finally, unsteadily, as if seen through a Bacchic haze, solo oboe recalls the Trio, but enough has been said and the only thing left is a final *tutti* collapse.

From the start of the slow movement it is evident that this Largo is to be a study in string sonorities. Violins are divided into three groups, and violas and celli into two groups each, as the reposeful first subject sets a mood of lyrical introspection in a broad paragraph of thirty-two bars which contains—at present hardly noticed even though the entry of the first violins is reserved for it—the *motif* with three prominent crotchets upon which the central climax is to be built.

A gently rising harp *motif*, giving way to a delicate ostinato, brings a flute solo which, in outline and mood, is related to the first violin subject of the opening movement, but thematic contradiction comes immediately from a second flute. The music grows in power as a rapt climax introduces the rest of the woodwind over a quiet timpani roll. A pause, then celli and basses draw attention to the violin *motif* quoted above: alone and proud, like a solemn pronouncement. A new theme on solo oboe emerges over *tremolo* strings, only to be taken over by clarinet to incorporate the three-crotchet *motif* which has once again been quietly insisted upon by lower strings. Flutes take over the oboe theme but soon give way to clarinets again over a rich bassoon accompaniment, after which the music is ready to move towards its great climax in which the composer uses xylophone to stress the three-crotchet *motif*. This leads to an extraordinarily effective example of scoring: celli, *fortissimo* and *espressivo*, take the descending oboe melody against constantly changing patterns of string *tremoli* punctuated heavily by double-bass quavers, *sfff*, the whole set against an agitated rippling effect on two clarinets in contrary motion. Upper woodwind and the three violin groups eventually add their weight to produce a rich and emotional texture of sound as the coda approaches. The music calms to a tense whisper after unwinding from the climax, and celesta and harp punctuate the last melodic line in an ending which strongly resembles in effect the finish of the Fourth Symphony.

The dynamic Finale literally bursts forth, a massive wall of sound to introduce the simplest and most straightforward symphonic movement the composer had thus far written.

This grand flourish resembles the opening of the Finale of Mahler's First Symphony: a sudden, rousing, electric sweep which leaves the timpani hammering out the precipitate rhythm.* Brass, completely silent in the slow movement, are now given the responsibility of announcing the positive main theme, and are greeted enthusiastically by shrill woodwind and affirming timpani. Soon, strings and wind whirl the music into a frenzy as the energies and tension pent up earlier in the symphony are released. The carnival atmosphere is intensified by several increases of tempi, at the last of which a solo trombone hurls out a new theme which, while in keeping with the mood of the surrounding music, yet contains elements of a greater nobility.

---

*The selection of a just tempo is vital if the beginning of the movement is not to sound coarse and inconsequential. Bernstein and Previn's earlier version lose much power by being too fast whereas Howard Mitchell is a shade too ponderous, even though his balanced performance allows the drama to unfold. Both of Ormandy's recordings and that by Ančerl are close to ideal.

The orchestration increases in brilliance, at one point the break-neck string semiquavers being reinforced by the sharp rattle of xylophone as trumpets and horns carry a whip-like fanfare figure. Strings then adopt the trombone theme, but it is the first theme of the movement that is proclaimed in hectic brass canon before, for sheer want of breath, the music finally calms.

Gradually, with benign emphasis, a solo horn reaffirms the trombone's theme over a heightening violin ostinato which crystallises into that same glorious melody, and in a pastoral episode of great delicacy the violins finally settle on another ostinato as lower strings and brass discuss various thematic elements of the movement. Harp assumes the violin ostinato as the development section closes. Recapitulation, as in the second movement, is a matter for considerable modification and in this case contraction. It starts softly, side drum marking out the rhythm as a timpani pedal establishes the tempo. Four horns and double bassoon add their own pedal as the first theme, trimmed and tempered, reappears and gathers momentum beneath an ever-rising chattering woodwind commentary, devolving to violins, soon to be supported by pianoforte as the volume grows. Neglecting the noble trombone theme, the entire orchestra is of one mind now, centred upon the brash melody which opened the movement but with a steadier tempo to give dignity and solemnity to the coda. Timpani take the foreground in the final march, literally to pound out the way.

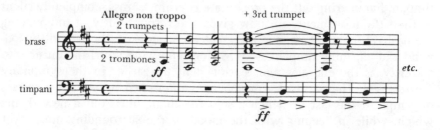

In the face of this percussive onslaught there can be no doubt: the artist has arrived.

Many critics wonder what would have happened to Shostakovich's musical development had he left Russia in 1936. It is an academic point, nationalistic, as were most of the writers and composers of his and preceding generations. His entire artistic development, training and creative force were geared towards his homeland. Art for art's sake was often secondary to the destiny of Russia in the view of many of the artistic *élite*, almost as a matter of tradition. Yet at the same time some artists strove to serve art first, or to use art to point out areas in which the government might bring change. They saw this as their duty to Russia out of the same nationalistic passion; artistic and expressive freedom were one major battleground. Shostakovich's Fifth Symphony was a document and a victory in this cause.

Igor Stravinsky, from his viewpoint as a nationalised American, once remarked that Soviet composers were good, but that they could not afford the luxury of integrity. Men such as Shostakovich, Myaskovsky and Prokofiev saw it not as a luxury but as a battle that should be waged at home because they believed in the government and its aims. Stravinsky, on the other hand, left Russia because his integrity would not allow him to remain. Shostakovich's symphonies demonstrate how far his integrity allowed him to go and how far he went.

Sixth Symphony (1939)

Shostakovich announced plans to create a symphonic tribute to Vladimir Lenin complete with choruses and magnificent orchestration. To judge from the composer's outlines the score would have emerged as theatrical, perhaps even embarrassingly banal. The symphony he planned might have resembled the Second and Third but with the advantage of the formal balance of the Fifth, or it might have become a hack work designed merely to endear the composer to his patron. Shostakovich obviously wanted to stay on the good side of the state (having experienced the bad side), and a "Lenin Symphony" would certainly have attained that end.

The project proved too massive. Shostakovich himself wrote at the time: "To embody in art the gigantic figure of this leader is going to be an incredibly difficult task . . . [I am thinking] only of the general theme, the general idea of this work. I have pondered long over the means of dealing with this theme in music. . ." Realising the enormous responsibility of his self-appointed task, Shostakovich decided that he needed more time to familiarise himself with his material in order to attain the proper attitude of mind. In the meantime he presented his

Sixth Symphony, produced perhaps as a diversion from the arduous task.

It is probable that the Soviet government felt that Shostakovich was stalling; but in fact the composer had come to realise that his plans for a "Lenin Symphony" were premature. As will be seen in the chapters that deal with both the Seventh and Eleventh Symphonies, when inspired on a grand theme he could work feverishly and earnestly, but evidently he had not brought himself to the mental pitch of concentration that he considered necessary to the successful fulfilment of the assignment, and when he had reached the required emotional and mental intensity the urgency to commemorate Lenin in music had given way to other matters. For the time being the Lenin project was postponed, but work was continued on it for two years, off and on, without tangible result, and when war broke out the task was shelved entirely.

The Sixth Symphony was not what was expected and was coolly received by both the state and the public. None doubted that it was a good work but many felt let down by it. For the most part the score avoids dramatic and heroic gestures, concentrating more on uncomplicated and beautiful aspects of the art. This symphony and the Twenty-First by Myaskovsky (1940) were taken as signs that beauty in art is good and necessary, and indeed still possible. None of Shotakovich's biographers has spent much time in discussing the work. The reason for this may be that the score offers neither a programme along the lines of the Second and Third, nor a triumphant affirmation of spirit as in the Fifth. Instead, it aims at a more modest target: that of providing sheer musical enjoyment for both musicians and audiences. The symphony was premiered at a Festival of Soviet Music in Moscow on December 3, 1939. It is arranged in three movements, using a tempo scheme of slow, fast, faster. Shostakovich was again experimenting with his symphonic plan, although in a limited way. The scope of the work is much smaller than any symphony since the First. We may speculate, however, that in the planning stage the composer envisaged a long slow, or moderately slow, movement to be positioned between the two quick ones. This would have given the work a more satisfying balance and would, furthermore, have presented an overall pattern similar to that used in the symphonies which lie on either side of the Sixth.

The opening movement is a long-drawn and stately Largo which, despite the composer's precise tempo indication of quaver=72, is open to a wide range of equally successful tempi in performance. When a very slow tempo is adopted, it is vital that the conductor takes a firm, concentrated line with the music that does not preclude flexibility;* and on the other hand, care must be taken if a faster speed is chosen that

---

* Adrian Boult's recording presents an outstandingly successful view of the movement at an unusually slow tempo.

the music does not sound too light and inconsequential. With these safeguards the movement works well at surprisingly divergent extremes of tempo. The first theme enters immediately on lower woodwind and lower strings:

There is strength and determination in the music, together with an undertone of tragedy. When the violins enter at bar 5 it is to announce an even stronger melodic line with an upward surging element (marked *a*) typical of the composer's questing urgency. Two horns in agonised triplets intensify the stress of the music before the violins, *piano* and *espressivo*, take *a* as an opening phrase for a further discussion of the material already heard. The lower wind instruments also examine this material, only to give way to violins, then piccolo, in succession. From the reserved scoring of the opening, the music has widened to include the highest and lowest voices in the wind section as piccolo rhapsodises over solemn progressions on double bassoon, the great central void occupied sketchily by an agitated second violin line in triplets. In danger, perhaps, of losing direction, the music is forcibly wrenched back to reality by a solo trumpet carrying the opening theme, and for a moment the brass stiffen the textures.

A solo cor anglais brings the second main subject (*poco più mosso e poco rubato*), less stern than much of the music heard thus far but still with an unmistakable resilience.* This *motif* in turn is gradually widened over a quietly trilling string bedrock until muted violins play the melody as if in deep awe, carrying it to an infinitely sad high B flat. One flute, later joined by another, takes the second theme into realms of breathless mystery in which the rest of the orchestra is, as it were, held in abeyance. The music moves deeper and deeper into unknown territory until, hesitantly and at first reluctant to leave the tenuous security of its first note, a solo horn leads the music back into the opening theme. The abbreviated recapitulation has arrived but it is a restatement of music which has undergone a profound transformation. Dark-toned wind (bassoon, bass clarinet, and two clarinets in their low register) bring about a brief recollection of the second subject on violins over trilling violas and sparse chords subtly marked by timpani, harp and lowest strings, and the music leaves the listener regretfully, as if aware of the possibility of being misunderstood but equally mindful of the fact that further statement can do nothing to elucidate this intensely personal and subtle declaration.

No greater contrast of mood could be imagined than that between the first movement and the playful restraint of the second. In a jaunty 3/8 rhythm of *pizzicato* strings, one of Shostakovich's favourite instruments, the small clarinet in E flat, announces the scherzo-like subject. Other woodwind join in and soon all the upper wind are chattering in *staccato* figuration in the well-defined rhythm; but curt interjections from all four horns cause the music to devolve on to strings in time for a second subject—smoother and gracefully rising, and moreover immediately acclaimed by a series of joyful whoops:

The horn punctuations are newly introduced and this time bring further rhythmic support from xylophone. Soon three bassoons discuss the above-quoted example in angular and accented tones that deny its grace,

---

* One will note the warning against too flaccid an approach that Shostakovich issues in his double use of *poco*.

but this is swept away by strings and then by swirling clarinets and the rest of the light woodwind as a quick climax finds the rhythm firmly delineated by brass and percussion. Four horns and three trumpets alternate in an exultant statement of the second subject. Quietly, the first violins play a subdued version of the same theme as a prelude to the recapitulation of the opening material on solo flute, accompanied simply by harp and lower strings. After the restraint of the first movement, the listener would be forgiven for thinking at this point that the movement was preparing to wind down to a *pianissimo* ending, but Shostakovich is now in playful mood and has much more in reserve. An extraordinary *motif* for bass clarinet and three bassoons, *forte, tenuto, espressivo*, over a pounding cello and bass line, brings renewed activity. This is the "trio" section, and a most forceful affair it is, too, invading the movement with its coarse character like an overbearing guest at a polite party. Violins take up its awkward syncopations amid antiphonal horn interjections, and timpani mark the rhythm with minimum subtlety, as if to draw attention to a basic time that seems in danger of being lost. Eventually a percussive climax arrives and timpani eloquently re-establish the opening mood and tempo of the movement. As before, this is carried for the most part by upper wind *timbres*, but its opening statement is on flute and bass clarinet in contrary motion—a daring trick which would have been unthinkable in the first presentation of this material but is now possible because of the liberating bad taste of the Trio. A new and fragmentary piccolo idea appears and second violins, answered by first horn, boldly produce the grotesque Trio theme. The memory of this haunts the upper wind for a space before the piccolo idea is restated, then transferred to celli and basses as a chromatic wind *glissando* closes the movement.

Criticism was levelled at the composer for writing two consecutive movements of a scherzo-like character. It is suggested above that the original plan was perhaps to place a contrasting slower movement between the Allegro and the Presto, a movement that has not survived or was used in another context. While it may be pointed out that the Allegro in 3/8 and in Scherzo-Trio-Scherzo form bears no relation to the Presto in barred common time and modified sonata form, the fact remains that the similarity of mood and tempo in two adjacent movements reduces the effect of both, justifying the critics' complaints.

The Finale is dominated by the opening violin theme:

much as is the Finale of Beethoven's Eighth Symphony, and in the sheer high spirits of the music this similarity is maintained. The opening paragraph of 137 bars deals mainly with the violins' opening idea, tripping along with abandon and interspersed with woodwind (and, once, two muted trumpets) in acclamation. For the second idea the time signature changes to 3/4 as two bassoons, double bassoon and double basses (a favourite Shostakovich grouping, but used here, *marcatissimo*, to establish the new rhythm with comically square-wheeled effect) prepare for a heavy but fast waltz for two clarinets and violas. First violins take over as the clarinets cease, and bassoons and horns join lower strings in a gauche off-shoot of the waltz. Three trumpets, *ff*, lead the music to a grotesquely swirling version of the dance that eventually collapses in a hectic passage of mutating time signatures: for 70 bars the music alternates between common time and 3/4, with one bar of 5/4 inserted for further confusion. During this passage a number of woodwind instruments are given important solos, notable among them being bassoon and piccolo. It is left to a solo violin to rescue the music from metric chaos, which it does by a simple return to the opening theme. The recapitulation has arrived, and its progress is fairly regular until it is time to reintroduce the clarinet's waltz theme. Now, however, the theme is transformed, "streamlined," into common time and played by four horns, *pesante*:

This is the formula required for the grandstand finish that Shostakovich has planned from the start. Woodwind, *staccato* over a heavy brass and percussion rhythm, and strings in their turn, try to steal the thunder of the horns' carnival tune, but they and the trumpets carry the music irresistibly towards a coda of exultant brass and trenchant timpani.

If the overall layout of the Sixth Symphony is ultimately unsatisfying, the work is still to be admired for its solid workmanship, intrinsically enjoyable content, and, in the fast movements, boundless wit. While these two movements display the kind of fantasy to be found in the first three symphonies, the long slow movement takes one step further the characteristic first heard in the opening and third movements of the Fifth Symphony: namely, the use of broad, timeless paragraphs of music, great planes of mood-painting applied to the listeners' consciousness as if with a palette knife. The ever-increasing time scales required by Shostakovich to build his atmospheric scenes are already reaching a peak and will be found at their most expansive in the next two symphonies and in the Eleventh. The consequent focusing of effort on one mood at a time must have cost the composer feats of concentration, and we are about to hear how he set about solving the task.

Seventh Symphony (1941)

When war came to Russia the city of Leningrad was besieged in one of the most brutal and courageous chapters of the war. Shostakovich, in Leningrad when the siege started, worked at a furious pace to create a tribute to his city and to the victory that had to come. The symphony formed a significant episode in the composer's life: it created of him a national hero never to leave the hearts of the Russian people, and its success prompted several authors to write biographies of him to show how he had progressed from the First Symphony to the Seventh. People wanted to know about the man. The symphony was also significant to modern music. "No composer before Shostakovich," wrote Nicholas Slonimsky, "had written a musical work depicting a still raging war, and no composer had ever attempted to describe a future victory, in music, with such power and conviction, at a time when his people fought for their very right to exist as a nation. No wonder, then, that the Leningrad Symphony became a symbol of the war effort, acquiring propaganda value in the most exalted sense of the word."

The Seventh Symphony is very Russian in mood and themes, very nationalistic, pent up with the invasion and the barbarity of the siege. Its contents depend upon the programme notes history wrote for it at the time. The score is possibly the most significant piece written since *Le sacre du printemps* because of how, when, and where it was written, and the response it received at home and among Russia's wartime allies. As an artist's personal statement it is of the highest calibre. Shostakovich provided a synthesis not only of war but also of all the things to be preserved by the struggle. It is beautiful music pointing towards beauty in the world and the challenge to that beauty.

The march in the first movement has drawn the most attention from writers, a simple melodic phrase put to massive use and transformation. The segment calls to mind many other composers. Béla Bartók parodied the phrase in his *Concerto for Orchestra* after hearing the symphony performed over the radio. Maurice Jarre borrowed the entire schematic idea to provide a dramatic setting for the film *Paris brûle-t-il? (Is Paris Burning?)*. Shostakovich himself may have borrowed the idea of a prolonged side-drum ostinato from Carl Nielsen's Fifth Symphony of 1922, and the abrupt phrase-endings recall those in the middle movement of Sibelius's Fifth Symphony (1915). Shostakovich would have doubtless known the Sibelius work but it is not certain that he had heard Nielsen's. If he had done so, it must have been during the thaw of 1924–8. The resemblance is striking, as are the visual resemblances between certain pages of the two composers' scores even when the musical and dramatic effects are dissimilar.

For the first movement the composer left an unequivocal guide for the listener:

[It] tells how our pleasant and peaceful life was disrupted by the ominous force of war. I did not intend to describe the war in a naturalistic manner (the drone of aircraft, the rumbling of tanks, artillery, salvos, etc.). I wrote no so-called battle music. I was trying to present the spirit and essence of those harsh events. The exposition of the first movement (Allegretto) tells of the happy life led by the people . . . such as was led by the Leningrad volunteer fighters before the war . . . by the entire city . . . by the entire country. The theme of war governs the middle passages.

But is it all as simple as it appears? Let us consider afresh the facts of the case and perhaps draw conclusions from them that do not necessarily tie in with the accepted provenance of the symphony. The opening of the first movement, the part designated by the composer as describing the "peaceful life" of pre-war Russia, opens with a robust, business-like string unison with stern trumpet and timpani punctuations, the whole darkened by the tone of two bassoons:

Melodically it seems earthbound and frustrated: notice the way bar 6 unexpectedly turns back to the opening, as if unable to progress and develop. The scoring, too, is serious and almost heavy-hearted. After an extended passage in which this opening mood is intensified and put under pressure by a growing number of dissonances, shrill woodwind cry out in anguish but are immediately crushed by low strings and wind:

When the temper of the music finally cools under a soothing flute duet, it is to make way for a violin theme that, if it is meant to portray the happy life of the people, sets about it in a most subdued and doubtful manner:

The ambivalent mood continues, piccolo imparting a somewhat spurious sheen to the music, the bass line making subdued ominous threats, and a muted solo violin closing the exposition with a pathetic question.

As if in answer comes a distant rattle of side drum, *ppp*, a dynamic level that is maintained for seventy bars, when it rises to *pp*. One of the most notorious and slandered passages in Twentieth-century music has begun, and a theme which is to remain for no fewer than 280 bars, unchanged except for dynamics and orchestration, is announced faintly on strings

over a side-drum rhythm that had started four bars earlier, and that endures for the whole of those 280 bars plus another sixty-six beyond that, putting a severe strain on the concentration and physical endurance of the drummer.*

Is this inconsequential march meant to depict the mindless hordes of Nazis sweeping towards Leningrad? Shostakovich claimed this was not battle music; we are tempted, then, to search for subtler meanings. From the viewpoint of the people of Leningrad conquest by the Germans may not have seemed such a bad thing *at first thought*, especially when we consider that Stalin always thought of the city of Leningrad as a hotbed of dissent, a trouble spot of independent thinkers. Shostakovich, then, may have portrayed the approaching army—from a Leningrader's

---

* A note in the score recommends that two or even three drummers should be used since one musician may not be able to attain the necessary volume of sound while maintaining clarity in the rhythmic pattern for the whole of the 350 bars.

point-of-view—happily, almost gaily in anticipation.* But as that army comes closer—as war in the abstract comes closer—Shostakovich shows how ugly it really is. The war theme takes on the spectre of an unstoppable, unrelenting force. And the people of Leningrad now know the truth: their lot is with the Soviet state. When Shostakovich finished the score in a "safe" place,† this movement could easily be seen as a demonstration of solidarity with the Russian war effort.‡

After the first statement of the 17½-bar-long march theme (first violins *arco*, but *secco*, second violins *col legno*, violas *pizzicato*), only the first part of which is quoted above, a tiny linking *motif* is heard (all strings, *pizzicato*, *pp*) and, as the march is repeated (solo flute, *legato*), a gently swaying syncopated accompaniment may be just detected, *ppp*, on celli. Earlier in his development Shostakovich may have been content to let this syncopated figure remain as a permanent accompaniment to the repeated march, but it is indicative of his artistry and bottomless imagination at this time that, as the flute statement draws to an end, he replaces the accompanying figure with another: basses and celli in imitation repeat a scrap of melody derived from the opening notes of the march, over which piccolo and flute intone the march yet again. An angular

---

* In his book "Babi Yar," Anatoli Kuznetsov, in sections that were deleted by the Soviet censors for the original publication but were restored in Jonathan Cape's English version of 1970, refers several times to the feeling of hopeful anticipation among the Russian people that the German invasion was to be a deliverance from Communism. The disappointment as the Germans also proved to be tyrants is reflected in this excerpt: "Ah, what a fool he is, that Hitler!" said my grandfather. "The Germans are not really so wicked. But he's made 'em into scoundrels. How we looked forward to them coming! And if only they had behaved decently Stalin would have been finished long ago. The people would be ready to live under the Tsar or under the rich, so long as it was not under Stalin. Then this monster turned out to be even worse than Stalin. . ."

† The majority of the work was written in Leningrad, but most of the Finale was composed after Shostakovich fled as a refugee to Kuibyshev in December 1941.

‡ It may be taken as an indication of the power and value of the music that this movement, especially the march theme, is still open to alternative interpretations, even after years in which its "meaning" has been accepted almost tacitly as a straightforward portrayal of the siege of Leningrad. Certainly Shostakovich himself left his meanings open to interpretation beyond the vague programme quoted on page 82. For example, the light beginning of the march theme may have been meant to depict, simply, that sense of adventure and comradeship in adversity that all men feel at the beginning of a campaign, only to see the transformation of the theme as the campaign lingers. A more straightforward interpretation would be of battle engaged and won, as the march theme is defeated ultimately by the very Russian theme—but the battle is not the war, and the march theme returns hauntingly at the end of the movement. Only in the Finale, then, is ultimate victory clearly envisaged by the composer. Robert Dearling has proposed yet another theory: the existence of a dualism in Shostakovich's purpose whereby, with the Nazis approaching and the outcome of the siege uncertain, the composer had in mind a score that could be interpreted favourably by whichever became the victorious side. There is no basis in fact for any interpretation beyond what Shostakovich wrote. It must be stated that any such dualism could easily have been erased before the *première*, and I cannot accept that Shostakovich could be so opportunistic at this point while remaining so Russian at every other juncture of his life.—RB.

rhythmic accompaniment divided between celli and basses supports the fourth appearance of the march: a loose imitation between oboe and bassoon; literally two statements in one. Piano joins the rhythm as lower strings continue their square accompaniment for the fifth appearance, now on muted trumpet and two muted trombones in harmony. Three horns snap out an ominous quaver as the march gains power, this time in close canon between piccolo clarinet in E flat plus clarinet on the one hand and oboe plus cor anglais on the other. The almost hysterical tone of the little clarinet brings a distinctly strained character to the march, and a sense of urgency is imparted by the hectic layering effect of the voices in the second half. The *staccato* accompaniment is now strengthened by low woodwind and brass as the march moves to violins. The texture becomes denser still on the next statement by full string band over an ostinato now intensified by the addition of timpani.

Xylophone now reinforces the rhythmic line as the march takes on a frightening volume, flung out *ff* by bass clarinet, two bassoons, double bassoon, lower strings and eight horns in unison. For the next statement a new ostinato is introduced: all the higher wind and stringed instruments reinforced by two horns and the celli play a tortured *motif* in ragged phrasing like the disorganised and desperate cries of an embattled nation

as two trumpets and two trombones, with harmonic support from a third trumpet and a third trombone, once more repeat the march. Both the new ostinato and the angular rhythm that had endured for several statements of the march now cease, to give way to an unbelievably ominous, swelling chromatic ostinato on all the lower instruments as the march appears yet again on all the higher ones, the orchestra split simply but effectively into two voices against the unchanging din of side drum, now joined by tambourine. For the twelfth and most raucous presentation of the march (five trumpets and three trombones with tuba), bass drum joins the side-drum rhythm while the rest of the orchestra is caught up in a succession of ruthless crotchets.

At last comes relief, at least from the march theme, as an inverted version

Allegretto (♩ = 116)

3 trumpets + 4 horns

fff

+ 3 trombones *8va* -

leads to some modest development. No relief is yet possible, however, from the pulverising weight of the side-drum rhythm and the cruelly marching crotchets of the rest of the orchestra, and chaos approaches as these crotchets turn to quavers and then to triplets in breathless diminution and fragments of the march theme are impelled around the brass section, xylophone and woodwind adding shrill tones to the combat. With chilling suddenness the side drum ceases its clatter and the whole orchestra, with a massive effort of will, struggles upward to a victorious plane in which the opening section is suggested. The crucial point in the battle has been reached at last, the victory is won, and thankfully the unbearable tension is reduced. It is left to a solo bassoon to sing the requiem for the dead before the first subject of the movement returns amid grief. The shrill woodwind cry heard so tellingly in the exposition (see p. 83) reappears for an instant in sudden fury, but another memory of the exposition, a consoling one on muted violins, draws the music to a close over a shattered and war-shocked people. Still the end has not come! The hideous rattle of side drum is heard again in the distance, signalling more to come; the battle continues.

After such a strongly programmatic first movement the rest of the symphony seems more "absolute" in conception, although the composer nevertheless provided a short description. The Moderato "is a lyrical Scherzo recalling times and events that were happy. It is tinged with melancholy." As a matter of interest, let us see how closely this non-committal commentary compares with the mood the listener will find in the music. The first theme is announced on second violins, a choice of scoring that throws immediate doubt on the avowed intention to recall happy times. There is, nevertheless, a certain quiet contentment as first violins join with seconds in a playful argument, but almost immediately comes a suggestion (marked *a*) of the shrill cry (see example on page 83) from the exposition of the first movement:

Moderato (poco allegretto)
(♩ = 96)

a

violins I

p

violins II

p

A touch of fantasy as violins take their highest register against a disagreeable bass line is short-lived, and soon the violins hesitantly adopt a quiet ostinato (already heard in the above example at the point marked b) as an agitated backdrop to a long and infinitely searching oboe solo, joined after twenty-six bars by cor anglais as two bassoons take up the accompaniment for two bars. Cor anglais leads the music into deeper meditation amid sombre tones from double bassoon. The last statement of the main theme before the Trio is for *pizzicato* strings, *piano*, joined by clarinet towards the end.

The key changes from B minor to C sharp minor for the Trio: a horrifying episode in 3/8 time,* the rhythm marked out vociferously by piercing combinations of instruments, oboe, cor anglais and upper strings later yielding to xylophone and piano. Against this the piccolo clarinet in E flat sings a grimacing dance of death, its manic *timbre* leading other wind instruments into a distorted waltz full of pain and stress. Two trumpets and a tuba introduce a meaningless fanfare, repeated several times as the Trio changes time and pulse again and again before finally disintegrating. Shostakovich was rarely given to understatement in his music, but if he felt able to describe this extraordinarily disruptive section as being "tinged with melancholy" it is evident that his verbal descriptive powers did not suffer from the same fault. At last the opening theme of the Scherzo returns, but far from being a regular statement it provides the composer with the opportunity for one of his most inspired strokes of scoring. Second flute changes to the contralto flute in G which, together with first and third flutes, provides an eerily fluttering complement to the searching oboe solo heard in the first part of the music—but with the solo now taken by the sinister voice of the bass clarinet. A coldly chiming harp provides a bare octave accompaniment, with occasional comment from self-effacing *pizzicato* violas. This example of chill desolation mingled with unexpressed dread must be one of the most gripping of all the colouristic fantasies of the Twentieth century, and one feels that the final statement of the theme, even though tinted again by the fascinating voice of the contralto flute, this time in isolation, is unnecessary—even prosaic. If Shostakovich had had the courage to

---

* Bernstein is perhaps the most successful on disc in giving vent to the underlying mood of this movement in his clear and forceful recording; other failings, however, prevent its inclusion in our Recommended Recordings list.

close the movement at the end of the bass clarinet solo, leaving that malevolent sound ringing in the ears of his audience together with the shimmering flutes, the effect would have been infinitely more telling.

"The third movement, a pathetic Adagio, expressing ecstatic love of life and the beauties of nature, passes uninterrupted into the fourth (Allegro non troppo) which, like the first, is a fundamental movement of the Symphony. The first movement is expressive of struggle; the fourth, of approaching victory." These words from Shostakovich's own written programme for the work do not necessarily mislead, as we may suspect of his comments for the first movement, but they continue his tendency towards understatement that we noticed in his remark about the Scherzo. Vast, static, glacial chords on woodwind and horns, supported by two harps, lead to a tortured declamation for violins against which impassive chords from the rest of the strings provide a harmonic bastion of sound, immensely strong yet featureless, like the pillars of a portico. The dual statement is repeated but the strings this time lead to a more grieving section for solo bassoon. Before the entry of this instrument, however, comes a phrase featuring a minim and two quavers which is not only similar in shape to one near the start of the slow movement of the Fifth Symphony (cf the example on page 70) but, as in that example, is presented almost as a by-product of the figuration, yet has about it an ear-grasping character and assumes structural importance later in the movement:

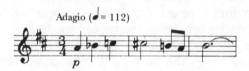

Celli and basses *pizzicato* stalk gauntly, but their rhythm is lightened as a solo flute seems to plead for less sombre times. Another flute joins this song as the music strives towards timeless happiness. Celli, then violins, take up this call for peace and security, incorporating the minim/two-quaver phrase, but the opening glacial statement is suggested quietly on lower strings, its appearance disconcerting the violins and forcing them into a passionate and strongly-dotted section over pulsating horn chords:

Trumpets, trombones and tuba now take over the violins' *motif* while all the strings pulsate, and all four horns in unison carry a noble theme which abruptly changes into the dotted *motif* over a side-drum ostinato. Three trumpets add their exultant voices in a section that seems to insist on the right to appreciate the glories of life at all cost and despite all outside evils. But it is the cold, passionless face of the opening chorale that grips the heart of the climax as upper strings and wind maintain a strenuous semitonal ostinato in the prevailing dotted rhythm. A crushing timpani roll brings the music to a lower level and trumpets play the *motif* first heard when violins answered that great icy chorale at the beginning of the movement. Recapitulation of the opening sequence eventually brings about a remarkable transformation as violas, simply and with great beauty, return to the flute melody with an ever more eloquent entreaty for peace and happiness. The opening dual statements, now exclusively on strings, bring the movement full circle with further references to the minim/two-quaver idea, and clarinet over a series of black wind chords brings the movement to a close. Three soft chords (timpani, tam-tam, and *pizzicato* strings) punctuate the lead-in to the Finale.

Barely heard over a timpani and string bass pedal, a violin theme emerges but is interrupted by a belligerent stirring of celli and basses. Like a challenge, a triplet figure is thrown between oboe and muted horn, and then the main business of the movement begins:

Energy and resolve are implicit in this determined melody, and the music quickly gathers impetus under an insistent repeated-quaver rhythm on woodwind, then trumpets. Most of the burden of the music is shouldered by the violins but the scoring becomes richer and thicker as divers elements are introduced. A section of scherzo-like joy is displaced immediately by an ugly and curt brass declamation, and a pre-cipitately rising-and-falling string idea is layered between running quavers against trumpet and trombone triplets. The Third Symphony is recalled here as the composer's imagination runs riot amid a torrent of fragmentary themes and rhythmic off-shoots. In a flash the music coalesces into a grand statement (woodwind and four horns) of the theme heard so tentatively at the very start of the movement, but as this ceases the supporting rhythm is left to carry the music into a new section in 7/4 of incredible drive and power. First violins are accompanied by *pizzicato* chords executed so violently that the strings rebound from the fingerboards. Two clarinets contradict this violin *motif* with such unexpected invective that it almost immediately loses control, skidding angrily to a halt on violas, *ff crescendo*.

A new section commences, *moderato*, hinting at the grim rhythm of the development section of the first movement. For a space this ghastly fragment of rhythm is contemplated in awe. Muted violins, *pianissimo*, recall a figure that had first been heard almost casually in the exposition of the first movement immediately before the piccolo solo:

but whereas the fourth note had previously reached A, it aspires now only to G:

Violins take up this theme, however, as the music moves from B major to C major, and it is destined to play a powerful part at the end of the symphony. The challenging triplet figure is heard as if at a distance, and the music grows in strength over continuous low woodwind quavers. As these move to violins and violas, striving upwards until adopted by four horns in unison, it is clear that the music is gaining power for the final celebration of victory. All eight horns repeat a fanfare-like figure over string and wind ostinati, and with all possible force the opening theme of the first movement is reaffirmed in dazzling triumph. The final three pages of the score require from virtually every player the dynamic *fff*, and when it is realised that the brass section alone comprises twenty-one players (eight horns, six trumpets, six trombones, and tuba) it will be understood that the conclusion of the symphony dedicated by Shostakovich to the brave and tragic city of Leningrad sets a new level in orchestral volume and impact.

Whatever the formal shortcomings of this work, one cannot deny that it produced the required patriotic effect wherever it was played in Russia, at the same time bringing the composer's name forward, in many cases for the first time, abroad. When Arturo Toscanini performed the symphony for the first time outside the Soviet Union on July 19, 1942, just twelve months after Shostakovich, trapped in besieged Leningrad, wrote the first notes of the work, the advance publicity surrounding the symphony ensured for the radio broadcast a vast audience,* but that audience was quick to melt away once the novelty of the work had exhausted itself. One of the reasons for this waning of interest may have been the great length of the work—at about seventy minutes the longest symphony the composer wrote. This extended time span must have come close to prolixity in the ears of some critics, but we should consider carefully before censuring the composer for it. The long passages of thinly scored material must have been designed for a purpose; they continue the characteristic that appeared in both the Fifth and Sixth Symphonies and which was remarked upon at the close of the preceding chapter. In the Seventh there are countless examples of long, sparsely accompanied solos for wind instruments (piccolo, flute, oboe, clarinet, cor anglais, bass clarinet and bassoon each has its turn), as if the composer is presenting to the listener one tone at a time and inviting him to study it, to appreciate its inner character, to identify with its very nature as it soliloquises on a given mood. Much the same type of effect can be heard in the folk music of Armenia and Turkey (as brought into the concert hall by Loris Tjeknavorian and Alan Hovhaness): primary colours are enthroned for the fascination of the audience—and

---

* That performance was recorded by RCA and has been available intermittently on commercial discs in both the U.S.A. and the U.K.

Shostakovich combines this technique with the wordless narrative style of mood-painting. Had he wished to, he could doubtless have made his "Leningrad Symphony" half an hour or more shorter by condensing his message as he had done in the Second and Third Symphonies, but he was in an expansive mood which required ample time in which to develop, and he obviously felt that the message he had to convey needed the utmost space for the maximum effect. We may criticise the first movement for its banal march theme now that we can see it in its true historical and artistic context, but perhaps the long desolate solos move on a plane of time occupied by Shostakovich alone.

As to the true meaning behind the symphony, that may well be another matter entirely : a matter for the individual listener to judge.

Eighth Symphony (1943)

When considering Shostakovich's symphonic output as a whole it has become the custom amongst commentators to regard the Seventh, Eighth and Ninth as a group, forming together what is often called the "War Triptych." It is true that the material in the first two works, and possibly some of that for the Ninth, was conceived during the war and that they form a logical progression of intention: the Seventh deals specifically with the horror of one battle, the Eighth examines more generally and introspectively the deep human suffering that war brings, and the Ninth looks forward to a bright future of peace and tranquillity; but musically the triptych is not so satisfying. The "Leningrad Symphony" is immensely long but often somewhat shallow in musical invention; the Eighth is rather shorter but more than compensates with its quality of musical thought; the Ninth is very short, notwithstanding its five movements, and for the most part light, if not actually inconsequential, in mood. It provides a poorly balanced end-panel to its two giant companions.

Considered in purely musical and emotional terms, a much more satisfying triptych is formed by the progression of Symphonies Eight,

Nine and Ten. Numbers Eight and Ten are of approximately the same size and emotional weight while the Ninth comes in central position like a contrasting entr'acte. In this grouping the Eighth may be seen as a profoundly troubled exploration of forces that are discussed at length, held in reserve during the high-spirited Ninth, then re-examined in the Tenth. The optimistic Finale of the latter may then be seen as a coda to the overall design in which a solution is found to the problems.

It is not suggested that the composer himself designed, or was even aware of, this emotional grouping, but the fact that his powers were at their highest peak during the ten years involved would seem to lend credibility to this plan. Never before the Eighth Symphony were Shostakovich's compositional abilities so sharp; and after the Tenth it was not until the Fourteenth Symphony of 1969 that he regained the same depth of concentration, although the special genius of those years lingered on in the First Cello Concerto (1959) and was transferred almost intact to the string quartets from the Seventh (1960) onwards. In approaching the Eighth Symphony, then, we reach the summit of his achievement in this form, a summit so exhalted that it is difficult to avoid language that would smack of hyperbole. Restricting ourselves to moderate language, we might say that, of all the symphonies composed in the first half of the Twentieth century, few approach the quality of Shostakovich's Eighth, Ninth and Tenth, and they are surpassed by a mere handful.

In comparison with the "Leningrad Symphony," the programme of the Eighth is much less concrete, its format, structure and ideas more abstract. It reflects the Russian ethos of 1943 in the midst of war: a numb sorrow mixed with anger and the as yet only dimly perceived hope of victory and peace. Help in the form of war materials from America and Britain seemed slow in coming, the longed-for Second Front had still not been opened by the Allies, and life revolved round the ever-present threat of death and destruction. In such an atmosphere the subjective mood of the music is no surprise. War thunders forth in the middle movements with unrelenting fury, the third movement being called a "Toccata of Death" by Martinov. The fourth movement's death drone, a simple lament of deep suffering, shows Shostakovich's depressed mood. As a whole, the Symphony seems to say: never forget our suffering, and teach our children well.

What is surprising in such circumstances is the high quality of musical invention. Shostakovich's debt to Mahler is again felt, but his own character is even stronger. The expansive opening movement, almost as long as the other four combined, is Mahlerian in conception, and some passages of the symphony have a *timbre* reminiscent even of Bruckner, but the listener will not remain for long in doubt that these influences, together once again with that of Nielsen, are put to work to produce music of a nature wholly typical of Shostakovich.

The ominous opening on lower strings

is unmistakably related to the leaping figure which introduced the Fifth Symphony:

It leads to the first theme, a long-breathed melody for first violins, with all the strings directed to play *sul tasto*—bowing above their fingerboards.

A

Shostakovich

Gallery

The rapt lines* intensify and are supported by two muted trumpets and doubled by two flutes. This is one of Shostakovich's great plains of music, evolving slowly and with a minimum of instrumental variety, a dialogue between violins and bass strings providing the entire musical interest. All the more effective, then, is the sudden entry of unsupported dark woodwind colours, gradually moving into brighter, if still sombre, sounds. The link to a new subject is effected by an ascending crotchet phrase on the flutes which fades out as strings, omitting first violins, announce a pulsating rhythm that again recalls the first movement of the Fifth Symphony. A consoling melody of grave beauty then appears on first violins. It becomes more ethereal as the violins divide into octaves, again *sul tasto*, and is then repeated by cor anglais and violas. Further discussion of the material thus far exposed is undertaken as strings explore its mood. Little by little, as flutes in their lowest register announce the development section over tortured viola and cello lines, the tension builds, timpani entering for the first time in the symphony with a derivative of the rhythm that accompanied the second subject. This rhythm, almost immediately switched to side drum, forces the music to a strident and dissonant climax. With the weight of the tragedy carried by powerful string and wind unisons, *ff*, the three trumpets call a repeated rhythmic figure. Then the four horns contribute a gradually ascending phrase in ear-splitting seconds. Under a rapid and apparently accelerating sequence for all the upper woodwind and strings, lower wind, tuba, celli and basses recall the rhythm of the opening notes of the symphony—a typical example of Shostakovich's black scoring, designed to obtain the maximum impact from his instrumental lines—and, high above, two trumpets intone a *motif* which seems to lie somewhere between similar important passages in the first movements of both the Fifth and Seventh Symphonies:

Abruptly the tempo increases to *allegro non troppo* (crotchet = 116) and a faster version of the opening phrase of the work is extended into a driving figure upon which is set a series of dramatic instrumental

---

* Kondrashin's performance with the Moscow Philharmonic Orchestra brings out this effect better than most, and where normal bowing is resumed, at the point at which our example stops, the gradually growing warmth of /the Russian players may be appreciated to the full because of the contrast with their foregoing veiled tone.

effects, notable amongst them being a strenuous cross-beat of four horns in six-time against common-time strings and woodwind triplets. We will have occasion to remember this telling device when we come to examine the Eleventh Symphony. Again the tempo increases (*allegro*, minim=96) and the battle passage of the "Leningrad Symphony" is evoked by brass over an inhuman bass of unvarying crotchets. This leads to the spellbinding climax of the movement. Reverting to *adagio* tempo, trumpets and trombones intone a distorted version of the first idea:

This is supported by rolls on timpani, side drum and bass drum with searing chords from the rest of the orchestra, including xylophone. Suddenly the terror passes, leaving only pain and anguish. Over *tremolo* strings the cor anglais commences a long oration in which, later, clarinet and oboe join for a space, lending strength to an impassioned climax. With a change to 5/4 time and to a throbbing string accompaniment, the cor anglais becomes more consoling, less accusing, and the argument is taken over by violins, then violas, and finally by basses. Before the end of the movement there is a moment of warning from trumpets supported by horns

but this fades and the music draws to a grey close with one final four-note trumpet statement.

The second movement, *allegretto*, is a war-like march, fast and powerful, alternating between sheer energy and play. It could have been intended as a heroic march calling forth the joy of being alive and optimism for the future, but if so it is still not a pretty picture. It displays Shostakovich's best biting, acid-etched orchestration, and it is very Russian in feeling. Prominent solos for one and sometimes two piccolos, bassoon, contra-bassoon and of course the piccolo clarinet lead the way; the orchestra thunderously follows. The coda of the movement rises from a deceptively placid interlude and ends with the timpani, *secco*, sounding three determined notes.

If the second movement takes the place of an unsmiling scherzo, the third is yet ten times grimmer. This "Toccata of Death" comes close to picture-music in its vivid description of a city, this time possibly Stalingrad (since renamed Volgograd), under shell-fire. Alternatively, as some critics of the time suggested, the movement may also be seen as the Soviet Army on the offensive, but the effect on the listener is likely to be the same: he will be made aware with utmost force of the unthinking brutality of war. Against a crushingly insistent crotchet beat that is heard in every one of the movement's 500 bars, the sickening crump of explosions and the pitiless whine of shells are depicted unmistakably in an orgy of exaggerated writing. Shostakovich obtains maximum ferocity by the use of countless forceful dynamic markings such as *sf*, *ff* and even *sffff* to ensure the utmost barbarity from the orchestra. It is a concept at once simple in design and yet of the utmost brilliance, and it puts an intense strain on the players, not only to secure the required force again and again in gradually increasing crescendi but also to maintain the strait-jacket discipline of the unremitting rhythm.* As a compositional exercise this movement is as daring as it is effective. The composer's inspiration was evidently at fever heat and his sheer endurance is breathtaking. A central section is announced in Russian tones by a solo trumpet:

---

* In André Previn's otherwise admirable performance with the London Symphony Orchestra, it is this movement that comes off least successfully, the players clearly finding difficulty in keeping to the fast pace that the conductor adopts.

It is answered by a side drum, perhaps depicting machine-gun fire. This interlude allows no respite from the pitiless hail of crotchets and it is in any case short-lived, the malevolent Toccata returning all too soon on muted violas, *forte*. Tension builds with amazing power, and as the rhythm is taken over by a timpani pedal, *ff*, the music prepares for its greatest onslaught on our senses: amid rasping seconds and sevenths, the rhythm is peremptorily cut off leaving a solo side-drum roll, *sff*, to bring about the fourth movement, which enters with *ff* strokes on tam-tam and bass drum.

This short movement is of vital structural importance in the symphony. After the *tour de force* of the Toccata it is necessary to lower the emotional temper of the work, and the composer uses a succession of favourite devices to achieve that aim. After the initial onslaught, brass and woodwind play an outline of a theme which gradually reduces the dynamic level. This outline is then played again by celli and basses as the start of a passacaglia. The earlier variations are all for strings and tend to merge into one another, but the fifth is a chastening horn solo, the sixth a piccolo solo that eschews any hint of the lightness and gaiety that instrument often brings. The seventh is for four flutter-tonguing flutes over *pizzicato* violins and violas, and the next is for two clarinets which take over the five-against-four rhythm of the piccolo. Once the clarinets have disposed of their variation they act as a kind of bell-like accompaniment for a richly harmonised string variation. Clarinets reign also in the tenth and eleventh variations, the latter leading, via some more ghostly bell-like figures, imperceptibly into the Finale. Miraculously the frenetic energy of the third movement has now been totally dispelled; the symphony may move at last into a more hopeful realm in which the stress of war, although still present, is subdued, and the promise of peace, although distant, is discernible.

In form, the Finale is a species of free variations. As in the last movement of Nielsen's Sixth Symphony (1926), the theme is announced by a solo bassoon, *allegretto*:

The accompaniment is for another bassoon and a double bassoon only. The first variation is for violins, the second for alternating solo flutes, and the third for celli over a *staccato* woodwind accompaniment once again recalls Nielsen in its gentle waltz-like pace. Notice in particular the segment marked *a*:

As this variation fades away on a held cello G flat a bitter blast of wind—actually two oboes—provides another *motif* that is to assume importance later

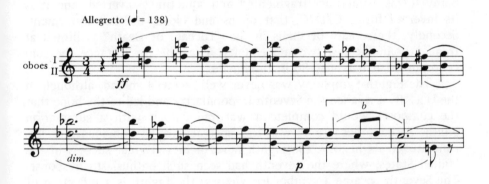

and which, at the point marked *b*, moves straight into variation four for oboe and two bassoons with, later, cor anglais. From the flute variation (two) the lower strings adopt a *staccato* line to accompany a flowing violin variation. The sixth is coloured by clarinet, bassoons and celli, swelling chromatically over three snapping trumpets; and the next variation continues the grotesquerie with strenuous double-stopped violin chords. All at once the violins quieten to provide a high-lying counterpoint as a fugue commences on celli and basses, gradually working upwards through the string voices, the oboes' theme quoted above now heard subtly in the inner parts. For variation nine the fugue is transferred to woodwind, two flutes playing the main melody against an oboe counter-subject. Further combinations take place in the eleventh (strings and horns against woodwind) and twelfth (brass and percussion, with woodwind increasing the tension); and in a fantasia-like section of heightened passion and accelerating tempo the music is precipitated into a gripping reprise of the chords which commenced the fourth movement after the halting of the Toccata. Ponderously, great chords are torn from the instruments as if in stricken remembrance of that moment, and trumpets and trombones strive upwards in dotted rhythm to a querulous progression which seems to insist that enough has been said about war and warlike things. The rest of the movement is a retrospective survey of the foregoing material, little by little bringing about a tranquil coda. A broad C major chord recalls the protracted end of the Fourth Symphony as lower strings, *pizzicato* and *vibrato molto*, repeat a three-note figure and celli bring final peace to the chilling oboe *motif*.

Those interested in finding the symphonic processes at work behind this remarkable piece are assured of rich rewards as they come to know and analyse the music. As in the best of Brahms or Sibelius, the music of Shostakovich's Eighth grows and develops within itself, tiny *motifs* giving rise to countless derivations. Two examples only will be noted: first, the C/B flat/C tag which opened the symphony appears later in many forms, sometimes fragmented and sometimes inverted, and it is its inverted form, C/D/C, that opens and closes the last movement. Secondly, the scream of shells in the "Toccata of Death" is hinted at frequently in the last two movements: examine for instance the solo cello phrase at bars 484–86 in the Finale.

The Eighth Symphony was never well received abroad, although in the U.S.S.R. it rivalled the Seventh in popularity and led to the hope that the composer would complete a wartime trilogy with a summation Ninth. Perhaps because it was less spectacular, less obvious and less romantic in its history, the Eighth never achieved great success in the United States, where the Seventh had seen such enthusiastic response. The Seventh became a symbol for victory; the Eighth is a reflection of a sad and burdened reality. As Martinov has said:

> The Eighth belongs to the number of those artistic creations, the significance of which cannot be at once fully recognised, which demand a considerable intellectual effort for their perception. It is very complicated both in contents and language. But the Eighth deserves such unusual concentration and attention, and to those who can penetrate its meaning, the Symphony has an unusual amount to say. It is a striking human document, a saga of difficult and glorious times.
>
> It is the quintessence of a great composer's art, the art of a composer who disposes with assurance of all modern methods of musical expression, and has mastered the unattainable art of achieving tonalities, unexpectedly novel and acute, by utilising the most simple—and apparently customary—means. It is necessary to stress this trait of Shostakovich's talent over and over again.

The Eighth Symphony was premiered on November 4, 1943, in Moscow during a festival of Soviet music conducted by Yevgyeni

Mravinsky. The score was dedicated to Mravinsky, the first time Shosta-kovich had ever dedicated a major work to an individual. Outside Russia, the Symphony received its first performance in America by the New York Philharmonic, conducted by Artur Rodziński, on April 2, 1944.

Ninth Symphony (1942)

When Shostakovich wrote his Ninth Symphony there was still current in musical circles a strange supposition that, when a composer had completed nine such works, he would progress no further. Had not Beethoven, Spohr, Schubert, Glazunov* and Bruckner all reached this fateful number,† only to be prevented by death from proceeding to the Tenth? And had not Mahler, in a paroxysm of superstition, refused to call his Ninth Symphony of 1908 by that name, seeking to circumvent fate by entitling it *Das Lied von der Erde*? Furthermore, when he did finally collect the courage to admit to writing a Ninth Symphony (the D flat of 1909), did not death intervene while he was in the midst of the next, thus tragically vindicating his fears? If, therefore, the Ninth was to be a composer's last symphony it was only reasonable that he should ensure that it was designed along the grandest lines with deep

---

* To the eight completed symphonies may be added an unfinished Ninth, two movements of which were completed by 1907.

† Antonín Dvořák may be added to this list, but only five of his symphonies were generally known in 1945.

psychological meaning so that it might stand as a worthy "farewell" to the world.

A lot of sentimental clap-trap, no doubt, built upon false mystical premises. Fortunately, this ridiculous superstition is rarely considered nowadays since several symphonists have nonchalantly sailed past the dreaded number, among them Alan Hovhaness* (36), Havergal Brian (32, plus an early and partly lost *Fantastic Symphony*), Nikolay Ovsianiko-Kulikovsky† (21), Henry Cowell (20), Gian Francesco Malipiero (17), Nils Viggo Bentzon* (14), Jiří Válek* (13), Allan Pettersson* (12), Heitor Villa-Lobos (12), Edmund Rubbra* (10), and Robert Lach (10). Mention should also be made of Nikolay Yakovlevich Myaskovsky (27), and it was perhaps to the example of this composer,‡ who had completed twenty-four symphonies by the end of the war, that Shostakovich looked when he started to write, fearlessly and without regard to the grim consequences, his Ninth. Certainly he ignored the tradition which seemed to dictate at that time that the Ninth Symphony should be an emotional work to sum up his aspirations and achievements, putting into it contents weighty enough to stand as his final testament, "just in case." It is possible that the composer regarded the Second, Third and Fourth Symphonies as lost causes and that by bowing to outside pressures which seemed to wish to forget the first two, and by allowing the Fourth to languish in silence, he felt that he might number to his credit only the First, Fifth, Sixth, Seventh and Eighth. This is an unlikely possibility. As far as is known, there has never been a move to re-number Shostakovich's symphonies, and certainly no hint that the E flat symphony of 1945 should be called the Sixth.§

It took Shostakovich considerable preparation and at least one false start to produce his Ninth Symphony, and when it finally appeared it was not long in meeting strong criticism from the authorities. Instead of celebrating the great and mighty Red Army in its victory, as the Soviet government wanted and expected him to do, Shostakovich decided to celebrate life and those things within the human spirit deprived men

---

* These are latest available figures for still-active composers.

† Almost alone in providing a large symphonic output in his time, Nikolay Ovsianiko-Kulikovsky is an early romantic composer who was born two years before Beethoven and lived until 1846.

§ If the symphonies *had* been renumbered during one of the composer's periods of self-doubt or insecurity amid the unstable artistic climate in which he worked, it is possible that the Second, Third and Fourth might have disappeared completely, depriving us of the opportunity of tracing his compositional development; the fact that the original numbers were retained for the later symphonies resulted, admittedly after too many years, in a healthy curiosity as to what those "missing" works might contain. We owe a debt of gratitude to the American conductor Morton Gould for giving the Western world its first recordings of the Second and Third.

‡ Myaskovsky, incidentally, beat the "ninth symphony jinx" in a novel way: his Ninth and Tenth Symphonies were composed simultaneously.

by war. The Ninth was the composer's own celebration of the end of the war. In contrast to the Seventh and Eighth Symphonies, the work is more laconic, very tight and neat, orchestrated with chamber-like restraint and purely classical in scope: almost Shostakovich's "Classical Symphony," in fact. In retrospect we may view the work as a sunny valley lying invitingly between the two grim peaks of the Eighth and Tenth Symphonies.

Once begun, the score was completed quickly. By August 1945 it was ready and Shostakovich remarked prophetically: "Musicians will love to play it and critics will delight in blasting it."

Martinov wrote of the opening movement: "This music contains so much vivacity and moral health, so much humour and inexhaustible joy of living, that it seems to be entirely woven of sunbeams and smiles." The second movement is elegiac, but even that grief is a song of beauty. In the fourth movement there is momentary respite from the overall festivity. Martinov argued that it is a brief moment of looking back and remembering—a poetic image common among wartime artists—before further celebration. Grigori Schneerson, a Soviet critic, wrote shortly before the score came under criticism: "The opening bars of the first movement transported us at once to a bright and pleasant world. There was joyous abandon, the warm pulsation of life and the exuberance of youth in whimsical dance themes and rhythms that remind us of Haydn. . . [the Scherzo] is music of radiant joy and almost child-like abandon to happiness." Subsequent adverse criticism was to pass, however, and today the symphony is one of Shostakovich's most popular scores abroad and at home.

The first of the five movements opens with a cheery theme on

violins abetted by solo flute and answered by oboe over a simple rhythmic accompaniment. In no time at all the busy strings round off the first subject and a brief pause clears the way for the second. This is a curious affair: solo trombone, *ff*, as if taking a breath, leads on an upbeat, and side drum supports with a coarse rhythm. This subject is the antithesis of the decorous first theme, and its widely spaced piccolo tune is pure slapstick. Three times the trombone lets forth its upbeat, but on the last occasion it is the trumpets and tuba that provide the tune. This is altogether too much for the rest of the orchestra and the whole thing is swept away with a curt gesture. Shostakovich then introduces something to be found in none other of his symphonies: he calls for a formal repeat of the exposition.* This is indeed a classical symphony in modern dress. As the first eighty-five bars are repeated, the listener may be forgiven for expecting the rest of the symphony to comprise a slow movement, a minuet complete with trio, and a concluding rondo. At the double bar the movement launches into a developmental sequence based on the first subject, its phrases being passed from group to group of the orchestra. Would that all real classical symphonies were so formally precise. Horns take bar three of the first subject but trombone deliberately tries to disrupt them by going in the wrong direction with the wrong rhythm, as if anxious to introduce its own theme once more. "If it is recognition you want," the orchestra seems to say, "here it is!" The piccolo tune is blurted out on full woodwind and brass, complete with side-drum accompaniment, and there is a sequence of brilliant, argumentative scoring as fragments of both themes fly hither and thither. The recapitulation arrives boldly, stamping string chords being set against a modified version of the first theme on bassoons, celli and basses. Immediately, the trombone upbeat interrupts, drawing attention to its own importance, but the music ignores it, reluctant to be halted in full spate and perhaps hoping that, if not encouraged, it will go away. No fewer than six times the trombone tries to find an audience for its piccolo theme, and since it is obvious that it is not going to give up, the orchestra stops in mid-stride. Momentarily disconcerted, the trombone quickly recovers, and with rude pride and assurance it invites the piccolo to play its tune, duly cued by the preparatory upbeat. But the piccolo is simply not ready and a solo violin has to act as a last-second stand-in. Regardless, trombone and side drum accompany the "wrong" instrument to the end of the theme, whereupon the piccolo, furious at being usurped at its moment of triumph, squeals its indignation. Too late! Clarinet announces the coda, loose ends are tied, and the movement is over.

The second movement is marked *moderato* without a metronome indication.† Solo clarinet soars in rapt D minor ecstasy over the simplest

---

* So far, it is believed that no recorded performance has adopted the barbarous practice of ignoring this vital repeat.

† Efrem Kurtz, in the first performance to be released on LP, took this movement at such an enormously slow tempo that there was no room for a reduction to *adagio* at the end, but such was the authority of his performance that subsequent ones at a more reasonable tempo often seem too fast. Most recorded performances capture the joy of the work but most have trouble in the transition to the more introspective passages. Bernstein demonstrates this fault most clearly. Koussevitzky's performance shows a balance as possibly ideal as one will hear.

possible bass-line. Another clarinet joins in and the two instruments carol together in sheer bliss. Other woodwind instruments join the song as the key moves to D major: flute, two oboes and bassoon, creating most delicate textures. A second idea, in F minor, enters on muted strings, and shadows drift across the tranquil landscape, but the woodwinds clearly disapprove of any factor that will mar their joy and the key returns to D major. Soon, however, clouds return, but they clear gradually and the strings help to bring about a tranquil close, the tempo dropping to *adagio* for the final piccolo statement of the opening melody.

The last three movements are continuous, but a classically-oriented listener expecting the first of them to be a minuet and trio will be disappointed. It is, in fact, a light Scherzo and the presentation of the first theme is once again entrusted to a single clarinet with sparse rhythmic support from two bassoons. Almost immediately a piccolo and two flutes join the clarinet, and two oboes join the bassoons, but this wind party is short-lived, violins entering with a rhythmic—rather than melodic—idea. A new *motif* is introduced: a prancing bass figure which is also adopted by woodwind over a violin counter-idea of drooping phrases that lends a diabolical energy to the music. This prancing, strongly-dotted rhythm quickly becomes the main driving force of the movement. It is even suggested in the central section of the piece, which is introduced by a rumbustious brass passage: trumpets, horns, trombones and tuba in a precipitate descent over timpani. The contrasting central section itself is announced by a trumpet solo over rushing strings:

Lower instruments (two bassoons, four horns, celli and basses) take up the trumpet's tune—their parts are incongruously marked *espressivo*— as side drum settles on the violins' rhythm.* An even more festive return to the Scherzo brings glittering new scoring to the same material, but unexpectedly the gaiety and rhythmic verve depart from the music, the humour slips away, and a great portentous statement from trombones

---

* In the Anglo-Soviet Music Press edition of the score (1946) this side-drum part is erroneously given to timpani at this point.

and tuba recalls a similar electrifying moment in the Ravel orchestration of Musorgsky's *Pictures from an Exhibition (Kartinki s vystavki)* at the point where the carefree bustle of Limoges Market Place is suddenly dispelled by a vision of the grim Catacombes deep below the streets of Paris. The fourth movement has begun.

This Largo comprises a heart-searching solo for bassoon strongly reminiscent of the post-battle scene in the "Leningrad Symphony." The challenging brass statement returns. As the bassoon repeats its sombre message the mood subtly changes: previously hollow string harmonies fill with warmth and—a wonderful moment*—the bassoon, almost in mid-phrase, slips slyly into the first theme of the Finale† :

Strings appropriate this portly theme, but their second statement of it is interrupted by an oboe with an altogether less friendly version. Eventually the two groups of instruments see eye-to-eye over the matter as a triangle marks alternate bars. A new string theme brings more weighty thoughts, but its seriousness does not last and as the exposition closes the sun still shines. The development opens with the first melody on bass strings combined with the second on clarinets, and for a moment the oboe tries out the trombone's upbeat from the first movement, but

---

* Beautifully natural and inevitable in Horvat's reading, but marred by much page-turning and fidgeting from the other orchestral players (or from the conductor?) in Bernstein's. (This latter recording is not listed in our Recommended Recordings list.)

† The Moscow bassoonist in Kondrashin's performance is miraculous here, and his treatment of the dotted crotchets of the new theme as teasing crescendi, although not marked thus in the score, is ideally in keeping with the spirit of the music.

it quickly remembers that it should be playing the second theme of the Finale, not of the first movement. The two melodies merge into one as the development moves underway, and as intensity increases the violins recall the oboe's unfriendly phrase and a certain amount of stress results. This is conclusively swept away by the recapitulation: a triumphant statement of the first theme on the weightier instruments, the rest of the orchestra joining the march. The remainder of the movement is totally free of problems: strings and wind chase each other up and down the first theme, fragments of it become ever quicker and shorter, and with a touch of good-natured percussion the Ninth Symphony is finished.

In this symphony Shostakovich turned his orchestra into a troupe of clowns, as had many an Eighteenth-century composer whose scale and forms he borrowed. It is easy to understand why the Soviet political machine, preoccupied with its business of clearing up after the war and anxious to launch into a programme of rebuilding the state for the future, found little time to laugh and had little patience with those who did. Musically the Ninth is a delightful and much-needed interlude of frolic after the gaunt edicts of the Seventh and Eighth; Shostakovich was not to lower his guard again in a symphony for another twenty-six years.

Tenth Symphony (1953)

By common consent the Tenth is the greatest of all Shostakovich's symphonies, both in the depth and balance of its moods and in the mastery of its techniques. As suggested in the introduction to the notes on the Eighth Symphony, all three works of the 1943–53 period are of surpassing quality, but there is little doubt that the Tenth, the second of two monumental peaks straddling the divertimento-like Ninth, is the finer of these peaks in many ways. Here is the heart of Shostakovich. In this work he opens his soul to the world, revealing its tragedy and profundity, but also its resilience and strength.

The birth of the Tenth Symphony came very hard. The composer worked on various projects during the period between the 1948 Zhdanov Decree and Stalin's death, but the serious side of his personality was expressed only in the fields of chamber and instrumental music.* The

---

* In this period, in addition to music for five films, the composer wrote two shallow patriotic choral works—The Song of the Forests (Pyesn o lesakh, 1949) and The Sun Shines over Our Motherland (Nad Rodinoy nashey solntse siyayet, 1952). His song-cycle From Jewish Folk Poetry (Iz yevreyskoy narodnoy poezii, 1948) was, like the First Violin Concerto of the same year, held in reserve until 1955. Of his more intimate works, only the Twenty-Four Preludes and Fugues, op. 87, was performed before Stalin's death. The Fourth and Fifth String Quartets (1949 and 1952 respectively) were reserved until the end of 1953.

long gestation period of the symphony may have given Shostakovich more time than usual to formulate, perfect and mould his material, and from this viewpoint, because the cultural climate was not favourable to the work until after Stalin's death, it may be admitted grudgingly that Zhdanov's inhibiting dictum was not necessarily a bad thing in this case.

The Tenth Symphony serves as a summation of the entire war and post-war period on Shostakovich's personal emotional plane, and then goes beyond that period. The composer himself said: "I wanted to portray human emotions and passions." As far as any specific programme was concerned, he would say only: "Let them listen and guess for themselves." Clearly, the symphony has no political or ideological programme. D. Rabinovich boldly draws a picture of a man versus evil *en force*, a kind of Straussian Hero's Life. Although Rabinovich carries the argument well throughout his discussion of the score, it is a tenuous offering, a contrived programme supplied to placate unsophisticated officials.

In the Tenth the composer appears to be reliving the emotions brought out first by war and then by censure. Restraint informs this reflective examination. The bright ending, reminiscent of that to the Sixth Symphony, is, in the words of Dmitri Kabalevsky: "The sunrise on the future." The work certainly does not come close to the image of Soviet realism that Stalin and the Central Committee fostered. It forces its audience to step up to its own level, offering no other guideline than their own personal response to feelings generated by the work, yet its musical language makes it accessible for the average listener so that he may comprehend that important things are being discussed.

The symphony was first performed under Yevgyeni Mravinsky in Leningrad on December 17, 1953, and was immediately a huge success, being hailed as a masterpiece both in Russia and abroad. It was then, and was to remain, one of his very greatest achievements, meeting with equal success the often incompatible requirements of accessibility and high musical value.

Apparently the balance of the work exercised the composer's ingenuity a great deal, despite what now appears as a simple and traditional layout. He returns to the slow/fast/slow/fast plan that had served him well in the Fifth and Seventh Symphonies, but he adds to the start of the Finale a transitional Andante that turns a good and well-tried format into an exceptionally satisfying one. Judged by a coldly analytical glance at the movements, the plan looks unpromising: an exceedingly long slow first movement is followed by a brief very fast one; another slow movement of medium length is then followed by yet another slow section which leads into the fast Finale, also of medium length. Fortunately it is the proportions of the weight of emotional content that are important here, not whether a stretch of music is fast or slow, and once the symphony has been absorbed by a sensitive listener, he will find that to contemplate the alteration in any way of these proportions would be to contemplate the destruction of much of the value of the music.

Arch-form has been employed frequently by symphonists to good effect: it is a simplification of the shape implied in sonata form and even in the emerging binary sonata form of the mid-Eighteenth century. Shostakovich chooses arch-form for his first movement and produces one of the greatest of all examples. Its span is vast, encompassing a world of experience. It is, at the same time, a truly symphonic movement in the sense that its growth is organic and its material integrated by the hand of a master of the art. Any commentary will fail in its attempt to describe the myriad subtleties, and it is with this fact in mind that the following notes are offered as a general guide only and not as a strict analysis. A written tour round the thematic mutations and evolutions may well deprive the listener of the satisfaction of personal discovery.

From the opening of the first movement it is obvious that Shosta-kovich is operating on his own protracted time-scale. Heavy with foreboding, celli and basses climb into audibility, only to slide back:

Violins and violas enrich the harmonies as a theme begins to emerge from the basic crotchet unit, but it is not clearly identified until a solo clarinet carries it tentatively against a wandering violin accompaniment. This violin line then adopts the melody and soon an element in quavers begins to assume importance:

This forces the music into a disturbed passage in which the opening crotchet idea is played in emphatic diminution by strings and wind, and inverted in semi-augmentation by horns. In a short chorale-like passage the brass reduce the intensity and the clarinet returns with an extended version of its first statement. Now it is time for the second subject. Solo flute against a *pizzicato* accompaniment insinuates a melody of sinister aspect, based mainly on a quaver pulse but incorporating the horns' inverted opening theme. Violins lead this flute theme into a new realm where it meets the instrument most suited to give it maximum haunting power—the clarinet:

This is played stridently by high winds, then a shade regretfully by violins as the exposition draws to a close.

Two bassoons and contra-bassoon consider two of the stated *motifs* over threatening drum rolls and the great central plain of the movement begins to unfold as closely woven fragments of these themes are heard. Prominent is the quaver *motif* on brass, the opening crotchet theme on strings, ff, *espressivo*, and at the height of the climax the horns' inversion of the opening notes; and after the main climax has passed there is a long section in which the quavers of both first and second subjects are combined. It is left to the listener to discover the amazing skill with which this climax is constructed from somewhat unpromising materials. At length the music subsides over bass quavers as the trombone and tuba chorale returns, once again introducing clarinet tone, but this time, instead of recalling the theme "rescued" from the darkness of the opening of the movement, two clarinets play the ghostly second subject in eerie thirds. Step by step the music seems to approach another climax, but apparently enough has been said and it remains only for a coda to bring the music full circle. A quiet timpani roll, swelling and subsiding between *pp* and *p*, brings numerous reminders of the crotchet phrase; then piccolo recalls the clarinet's first theme over second piccolo in even crotchets. With infinite regret, first piccolo closes the movement.

After the delicate sounds of the end of the first movement, the Allegro enters with shattering effect. Of only four minutes' length, it is exaggerated in everything except duration. The most frequent and sustained dynamic indication is *ff* (in a total of 360 bars, only 42 towards the end fall in intensity to *piano* or below), and the headlong tempo is unremitting. It is a whirling fireball of a movement, filled with malevolent fury. As a vision of concentrated diabolical venom it is unique. With such volatile music in his mind, it is certain that the composer envisaged some extra-musical picture, but since he did not specify what it might be the listener is free to affix whatever programme he chooses. With irresistible energy the movement opens on strings, and as they continue their *staccato* rhythm oboes and clarinets enter with a figure designed to propel the music at a prodigious pace:

Side drum contributes its hectic rattle and horns and trumpets lend weight and brilliance, but at the end of the movement it is the impetuous higher strings and woodwind that possess the listener's memory.

Just as the great march movement in Tchaikovsky's Sixth Symphony makes a fine stirring effect which is even so somehow inconclusive, so

the second movement of Shostakovich's Tenth Symphony needs something contrasting to follow it, something to lower the tension and calm
fevered senses. Tchaikovsky chose a despairing Adagio but Shostakovich
is altogether more optimistic in his choice, although this is not
immediately apparent. The Allegretto opens with a gently rocking theme
on strings*:

Second violins enter in canon. Then, over *mezzo piano* timpani chords,
two clarinets bring a new idea: a species of toy march on high wind,
introducing the DSCH *motif* we shall meet again in a few moments.†
Violins pick up the march idea at a higher level, but flute, over clarinet
harmonies, returns the music to the relative security of the first theme
and bassoon, with *pizzicato* strings and quiet percussion, forms a link
to one of the most breathtaking moments in all music. Celli and basses,
almost as part of their accompaniment, play the four-note DSCH theme:

The appearance of the phrase at this point is of high significance,
standing as it does immediately before the gripping entrance of an
imperious statement for solo horn, *forte*:

---

* This idea has already been used, much faster, in the Scherzo of the First Violin
Concerto.
† This sequence forms Shostakovich's musical monogram, standing for his initials
in German transliteration: Dimitri SCHostakowitsch (= D, E flat, C, B natural).

It is as if the composer is saying with his signature: "This is the true Shostakovich speaking. Listen to what I have to say!" The Tenth Symphony is not scored for vocalists and the "meaning" of the music is not vouchsafed by the composer, but there can be no doubt that this sonorous horn call is a warning, like a remonstrating finger of God held up to mankind. Amid a spellbound silence the call comes again, softer and more consoling*, and the lower strings answer with the opening phrase of the first movement. Again and again comes the call as the rest of the orchestra tries various answers in attempts to justify its existence, but the horn call remains unblinking and impassive, uttering its solemn exhortation. At last, cor anglais returns to the main theme of the Allegretto and for a space the orchestra is preoccupied with this idea even if it seems still ill-at-ease, as if living on borrowed time. The toy march returns and leads to a curious distortion of the first theme which quickly builds to a titanic climax, the DSCH *motif* repeated over and over by strings amid hammering rhythms from the rest of the orchestra.† At the height of this conflict, on four horns, *ff*, the terrible warning sounds out again and gradually the music collapses like a deflating balloon. Quietly, as if dispassionately surveying the wreck, the horn call returns yet again, to be answered by a solo violin, muted, with the first theme of the movement, and by *pizzicato* basses with DSCH; and after a final recollection of the horn's admonition the movement closes with the thrice-repeated DSCH signature on *staccato* piccolo and flute.

The opening of the Finale, in E minor, is marked *andante* and, as in the first movement, it heaves into existence on celli and basses:

Oboe sings a doleful song which, after a brief pause, rises and falls from G sharp in a plaintive wail, and flute takes over the lament:

---

* The solo horn player is required to produce a wide range of expression in his successive statements. Too even and similar deliveries give a prosaic result. This is the only real drawback of Andrew Davis's otherwise excellent recording of the work.

† No more thrilling affirmation of the composer's personality could be imagined. It is almost vocal in its eloquence, the composer's own voice rising triumphantly from the surrounding clamour.

Piccolo answers briefly, and the opening phrase is repeated on low strings. A sharp *pizzicato* punctuation brings a long bassoon solo; oboe twice repeats its plaint, which is extended by flute, then by piccolo, and a new melody begins to crystallise on clarinet and flute, rising a fifth at first and gradually extending itself. Abruptly the tempo changes to *allegro*, the key to E major, and this searching *motif*, suddenly relieved of its wistful quality, is announced in full by violins:

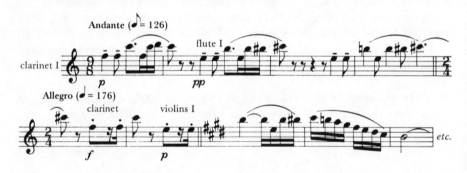

The now-joyful theme is tossed to the woodwind, then back again to strings. A marching *motif* on strings with off-beat support from horns and trumpets holds the limelight for a while as a second subject group, and it runs into some very Russian-sounding working out. The intensity and turbulence of the music grow rapidly, the whole orchestra caught in the rush. Unexpectedly there is a hint of something dimly familiar; but by the time the mind has grasped the fleeting reference as a quote from the opening of the third movement a far more terrifying reference occurs: suddenly the whole orchestra capitulates to the diabolical second movement. With volcanic force the music splits apart at this evil intervention and the whole orchestra hurls out one single protesting, crushing, statement of DSCH, supported by timpani, side drum, cymbals, bass drum, and tam-tam. It is as thrilling a moment as any in music: one may picture the composer progressively losing control of his music only to reassert his personality with a titanic force of will. A brief return to the slow introduction of this Finale leads to a resumption of the rhythm of the second movement, *mezzo forte* on low strings, against a quiet trumpet/trombone hint of DSCH. High woodwind recall the oboe's wailing phrase, muted violins and violas again invoke the slow introduction in misty *divisi*, and an unexpected rhythm commences on percussion. This brings happier sounds: a bassoon in garrulous mood repeats the main theme, and as that instrument loses its way in a tangle of quavers a clarinet illustrates how it should be played. First and third horns, with dynamic effect, copy the bassoon, as if to justify its attempt, but they run straight into DSCH. The music looks set to build again to a climax, but the mood is steadier, control firmer—so firm in fact that at the instant a side drum enters with the threatening rattle of the second movement, four horns counter-attack with six searing statements of DSCH in increasing diminution and trombones and tuba lend support in enormous augmentation. The composer, if we choose to interpret his music in this way, has won his battle against the forces of evil. There can be no doubt about his victory as the musical signature DSCH is pounded out six times *fortissimo* by timpani in the closing bars amid a blaze of triumphant E major.

Examination of the foregoing musical examples will reveal that the composer seemed preoccupied with the idea of three initial rising notes, but of much greater importance is his employment of his ego-symbol, the figure DSCH. The use of a personal musical motto was by no means new, of course. Bach had employed the phrase BACH (=B flat, A, C, B natural) and Schumann had added the initial of his second christian name, Alexander, to the first three letters of his family name to produce ASCH (=A, E flat, C, B natural).* However, no composer ever used it with such insistence as Shostakovich. It appeared in his First Violin Concerto (1948/48), in some ways a companion work to the Tenth Symphony, and in 1960 it was to become almost the sole melodic content of the Eighth String Quartet. As a self-contained unit of four notes it is satisfying, if tonally ambiguous, and it gave rise to related four-note *motifs* in the First Cello Concerto (1959), the Second Violin Concerto (1967) and the Fifth (1954) and Seventh (1960) String Quartets. The dates of these appearances are perhaps significant. Its first prominence coincides with Zhdanov's criticisms in 1948, and its use reached a peak in 1960. This is the very period during which the composer would have been most concerned to establish and assert his own personality, at first covertly, and then, with the death of Stalin and the world-wide acclaim of the Tenth Symphony, with utmost self-assurance.

---

* Mozart's so-called "Jupiter theme"—CDFE—although not encoding a personal identification, similarly fascinated him throughout his life.

Eleventh Symphony, "The Year 1905" (1957)

If we are deprived of a programme for the Tenth Symphony, the Eleventh makes amends by bearing the most precise programme Shostakovich had thus far supplied for a symphony. Nevertheless, his treatment of this programme remains less literal than sensual. The sincerity of his effort does not come into question. One need only mention the subtitle, "The Year 1905," to elicit a chill from any Russian student. This was the year of the fiasco that was the Russo-Japanese War, of Bloody Sunday, of the first Russian Revolution, of the beginning of the end for the Romanov dynasty. It was the year that Russian factory workers at last proclaimed that their conditions were intolerable and that outlawed strikes were their only hope. It is said that if a Russian was not sympathetic to the cause of revolution before 1905 he was sympathetic after it. Shostakovich, born in 1906, undertook the task of capturing that moment's emotional appeal. He did so in a highly romantic score with modern drive, nervous energy and a firm grip on architectural design within an immensely expanded time-scale. In doing so he created a Soviet Heroic Symphony. His subject came straight from Russian history and his music was based on folk and revolutionary songs which grew from that history. The style of the music was conservative, with mass appeal, and the work's popularity became very localised, even though for its colour and power it attained a wide if sometimes grudging appreciation. It is the subject of the abortive 1905 Revolution that gives the Eleventh its strength, but this programme earned it scorn among Western critics. If the nature of its programme had been withheld from these critics they would doubtless have invented one, but it is unlikely that a scenario dreamed up by the most inept of critics would have damaged the reputation of the symphony in the West as much as the one actually published for it. How can a commentator who is out of sympathy with the message of the work appreciate just how well that message is conveyed? Whether we "approve" of the Russians, their revolutions, and their policies, we must recognise the meaning of those things to a Russian, and our business here is with art. In the case of the Eleventh Symphony, the art came about entirely through the political happenings of fifty-two years earlier, and we are obliged to take those events into consideration when discussing the music. In truth, the music does not stand up without its supporting segment of history, but *with* it, it stands proud and commanding. It does triumphantly well what it sets out to do.

Since the programme of the symphony is so vital to our understanding, it behoves us to examine those events. In fact, the segment described fits neatly with the four-movement (slow/fast/slow/fast) scheme that the composer had evolved in earlier symphonies. In Nineteenth-century Russia, for every member of the *élite* in the ruling class there were thousands of peasants and factory workers hopelessly oppressed by tax burdens and the inefficient economic policies of the tsars. The complaints and proposals for reform put forward by the proletariat were not heard, or if they were they were answered by force. The common man was kept in his place at the very bottom of the structure of society by the simple means of allowing him no rights apart from the right to work hard for long hours so that the *élite* might benefit. The peasants' only pleasure was in folk music: a tragic and lonely art often with a feeling of hopelessness.

In the first movement of his symphony Shostakovich draws on this folk music to depict the people, chilled and hungry, waiting for bread in the square outside the Palace. The second movement is entitled "Ninth of January," that day in 1905 which is known to Russians as "Bloody Sunday."* On that day a large group of peasants and workers made a protest march carrying ikons and singing religious songs to the Winter

---

* The 1582 Gregorian calendar was not adopted by the U.S.S.R. until February 14 (1 in the old style), 1918. The Sunday in question, January 9, 1905, was January 22 to the rest of the world.

Palace in St. Petersburg. The tsar was not there; the marchers thought
he was. Instead, they met a detachment of Cossack bodyguards who
promptly opened fire on the protesters, perhaps mistaking their ikons for
weapons and their hymns for revolutionary songs. The Cossacks then
rode down on the people, brandishing swords. A thousand unarmed men
died in the snow. Shostakovich captures that horrid moment starkly,
in one of his most astonishing orchestral displays, yet the combative
episode is restrained, with a well-woven build-up to the actual con-
frontation and a sobering, beautiful aftermath of quiet, utter sorrow.

The third movement, "Eternal Memory," is a requiem for those who
died on that day. It has no specific historic relevance apart from the
eternal tragedy which is the fate of the Russian people. For his Finale
Shostakovich constructed a grim warning entitled "The Alarm" (tocsin).
In it, he says that, although the march of 1905 was a tragic error, the
reasons for it remain. Resentment and bitterness will one day boil over
and engulf the guilty ones.

Although the Eleventh Symphony takes almost an hour to traverse
this simple plan, there is a remarkable restraint and conciseness about
the musical language which ensures that the message is delivered with
the utmost clarity and the minimum of clutter. The great acreages of
slow music in the first and third movements contribute positively to their
respective pictures, the one conveying the endless years of waiting for
justice, the other the numbed grief of the nation for the slain victims
of the ill-considered uprising. Shostakovich also requires ample time to
build his faster movements: to portray the resolve of the marchers
and the means by which they are overcome, and to create the slow
resurgence of resolve and trust in the future which he depicts so vividly
in the Finale. Perhaps the events he describes move slowly but, because
he always has one more dramatic stroke in reserve, the total effect of
the work is overwhelmingly moving.

When we examine the symphony in more detail we will discover
just how skilful is the composer's deployment of these dramatic devices.
The first movement, *adagio* ("Palace Square"), opens immediately with
a vague, uneasy melodic line which is to serve as an *idée fixe*:

Harp chords toll like the passing of great spans of time. Against this
hushed backdrop the timpani mutter discontent

and trumpet answers with a subdued message of hope, like a distant
rallying call:

The cycle is repeated, a muted solo horn taking up the trumpet's call.
An extension of the opening string theme is to assume importance
later in the symphony and is quoted now for reference:

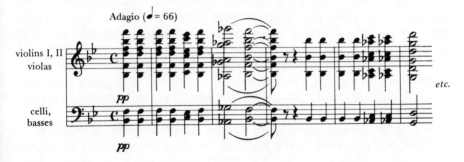

From the timpani triplets emerges a flute tune, a second flute harmonising. This is the people's song "Listen," and it is soon taken up by trumpet over a distant side-drum rhythm. Further statements of the melody are made by four muted horns, *mf*, bassoon, violins and violas, then violins alone; in the meantime the basses have introduced another song, "The Convict," and elements of the two songs are mingled. Eventually the *idée fixe* returns, together with its concomitant timpani rhythm and trumpet calls, and the movement closes with references to the extension of the *idée fixe*.

The second movement ("Ninth of January") opens with the theme "Bare Your Heads" from Shostakovich's *Ten Poems for Chorus on Texts by Revolutionary Poets* (1951), announced by lower strings and immediately augmented by clarinet and bassoon. Only bars 11–13 of the movement are quoted here

and, as we are coming to expect from Shostakovich's handling of his material in this symphony, the theme is rarely absent. At first the music seems to experience difficulty in moving under way, but the augmented version lends impetus and the music quickly gathers momentum until the whole orchestra is involved. The trumpet call from the first movement is answered by horns and it seems that nothing can resist the forward surge of the movement. Trumpet, three trombones and tuba intone a hymn-like *motif* as timpani and side drum, then timpani alone, maintain an insistent quiet triplet rhythm. "Bare Your Heads" is heard again on violins. Shrilly, in violent cross-rhythm (six against three), woodwind increase the tension, their chattering taken up by other instruments. The swaying music gathers yet more strength, but amid grim warnings it seems to go temporarily out of ear-shot. Suddenly, the *idée fixe* is reintroduced. Now, however, it is tight-lipped and determined: this is the final call for compassion as the crowd of disorganised workers stands facing the Palace, awkward, foolish, awed, as if waiting for some sign of mercy. The trumpet call is sounded.

As if in answer there is a rattle of drums. Cossack guards make a belligerent appearance, more and more of them materialising in a tense fugue to confront the crowd. They open fire. Once the initial shot has been fired there is nothing anyone can do to stop the bloodbath. In a withering passage of stark horror, Shostakovich draws the scene of red and white in a compelling episode of cross-rhythms, four against three, as the mounted Cossacks lunge forward with their swords, cutting lanes of agony and death through the host of pathetic humanity. The listener is spared nothing.

Prominent in the massacre scene, the four-against-three device brings to mind a cardinal point in the first movement of the Eighth Symphony, where the rhythms were four against six. Few musical tricks bring a more disruptive effect, and when, as here, it is employed at top dynamic level and over a vast span of music one must only marvel yet again at the composer's courage and the correctness of his judgement.

In an instant the carnage is over, the *idée fixe* left hanging in the air like a drifting mist:

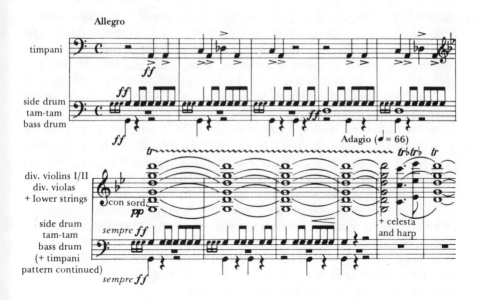

In blank disbelief, the music quivers with shock, contemplating the scene of death; but one thing still lives: in the distance is heard the trumpet call, muted now but still resolved. Its important extension returns on bass clarinet, contra-bassoon and muted brass. The song "Listen" also returns, but its ending sags in sorrow. Celesta and harp recall "Bare Your Heads," timpani mutter a warning, and the movement ends in despair.

The third movement ("Eternal Memory") actually starts one bar before the veil-like string harmony ceases, but for our purposes it may be said to open with a series of quiet *pizzicato* chords which introduce the song "You Fell as Victims." This is presented on the rich beauty of violas against the *pizzicato* accompaniment of celli and basses and is allowed to run its course, upper strings gradually joining the lament. Twice, sadly bringing to mind the second movement's tragic climax, violins play a triplet figure which is suddenly seized by low clarinets and low strings as an adjunct to a quiet brass funeral chorale. In remembering our dead comrades, the music seems to say, let us not forget how and why they died. By degrees the funeral song grows in indignation, the resurgent triplet rhythm insisted upon by brass and drums. The struggle is to continue with renewed strength, but before it can do so the fallen victims must be honoured once more.

Without warning the tocsin is sounded as a commanding fanfare (fourth movement). Its outline has a family resemblance to the slow opening of the Finale of the Tenth Symphony, and we are to meet another close relative in the Fourteenth Symphony to depict a doomed soldier boy. Here, the biting earnestness of the music is unmistakable as celli and basses in unison take up the powerful *staccato* rhythm. The tocsin returns with greater power and upper strings join the march. Interjections from *staccato* woodwind, brass and timpani marshal the growing power of the cause; shrill woodwind proclaim their support as courage, resolve and arms are assembled in a dazzling crescendo of orchestral colour. Suddenly the whole force is marching resolutely. For some two hundred bars the music swells with a purpose as unyielding as volcanic lava, the frequent block unisons indicating the unanimous support of the people for the cause. In this truly breath-taking feat of concentrated writing, Shostakovich reveals the strength of a master of emotional appeal. No stops remain unpulled. Every device is included to elicit maximum audience response: the trumpet fanfare is sounded in close canon, and the "massacre triplets" remind the listener of the motive behind this fury, energy and resolve. Amid the stentorian sounds of a revolutionary song the music reaches a stupendous climax, the unbearable tension at last released by a series of references to the tocsin and a stroke, *fff*, on cymbals and bass drum.

We are in the Palace Square. Cor anglais sings a lament:

The sad history of Russia is summed up in this song, but, with the hope of a bright future, the people of the Revolution are now ready, organised and armed, awaiting their moment. "It could have been so different had you listened," the music seems to say, "but you turned your back. You leave us no alternative." The music changes to *allegro* amid incisive strokes on bass drum and tam-tam. The opening theme of the second movement is heard, gabbled out with the utmost evil effect by bass clarinet. It is almost as if that instrument had been designed with this moment in mind: no other could have brought such sinister expression to the moment. It leads to a hurtling passage for all the winds in confusion, a rushing figure taken up by strings as yet again the music grows in vehemence. As the end approaches the emotionally exhausted listener is subjected to yet another of Shostakovich's most dramatic strokes as the coda enters over tenacious side drum and timpani: the cutting but baleful *timbre* of chimes. A repeated G drops eventually to C, rises to B flat and B natural, and in the final bars the bells are the dominant sound in a skeleton of a *motif* that sums up the whole symphony. This is not an overtly triumphant ending—after all, there is little to be triumphant about in a failed revolution—but its message cannot be doubted: "We shall return."

Twelfth Symphony, "The Year 1917" (1961)

The Twelfth Symphony is closely related to the Eleventh in that its movements are played without pause and its programme is inspired by revolution. The composer goes one step on from 1905 to portray the successful Bolshevik Revolution of 1917. More importantly, he portrays the leader of that revolt and seems to look at the event through Lenin's psyche. It will be remembered that Shostakovich planned a "Lenin Symphony" in 1938 but those plans were pushed aside by the far more pressing events of the Second World War. With the war over, Stalin gone, and Shostakovich having reached a remarkable peak of purely musical intensity in the Tenth Symphony, and, furthermore, the painful 1905 Revolution duly commemorated in the Eleventh, he was ready again to tackle the subject of Lenin. Unlike the elaborate Eleventh, or even the grandiose plans he outlined initially in 1938, however, the music dedicated to Lenin does not take on an expanded form, although it is not free from a certain gratuitous bombast. Overall, the score is conventional and does not use genuine folk material. After the effective exploration of the Soviet ideal in the Eleventh, Shostakovich apparently felt that it would be ignoble to duplicate the canvas. Instead he chose a

Above: Shostakovich with Kabalevsky and Khrennikov
Below: Shostakovich with Mstislav Rostropovich

Above: Shostakovich with his son Dmitri
Below: Shostakovich with Dmitri and David Oistrakh

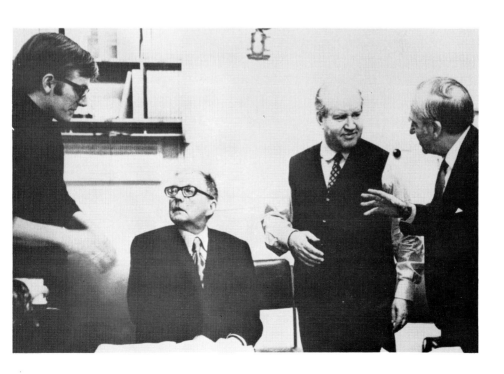

tighter perspective, relying on only two themes to dominate the whole work. As an experiment in economy it is notable, but of all the symphonies the Twelfth is, perhaps, the least convincing.*

As in the Eleventh, this work indicates its programme in the title and in the subtitles of the four movements: I: "Revolutionary Petrograd," setting the stage; II: "Razliv"; III: "Aurora"; and IV: "Dawn of Humanity," demonstrating the true beginning of the new Soviet Union with a youthful resolve. The meanings of the names of the central movements will become clear in the commentary that follows.

The music is easily accessible, more proletarian than any other of his symphonies, but less permanent. Only the scherzo-like third movement shows any uniqueness—an episode in what is for Shostakovich an unusual position for such a movement. The Twelfth is over-orchestrated, a sign of the composer's possible discomfort with his material, and the Finale is unduly long. Moreover, the thinness of the invention indicates that the subject matter was, perhaps after all, too uninspiring for Shostakovich. The Twelfth Symphony does not succeed as a sincere work, and as part of his symphonic output it has neither important place nor outstanding interest. Furthermore, it seems more contrived than any other symphony Shostakovich presented, and it needs an outstanding performance of a committed interpretation to make it work.

The first movement, "Revolutionary Petrograd," begins, *moderato*, with a grimly determined figure on lower strings,

widening in steps as first the upper strings, then some woodwind and horns, and finally the rest of the woodwind, together with trumpets, trombones and tuba, hesitate on a four-fold presentation of an anticipatory figure. It will be noticed that, as Boris Schwarz has pointed out, the music has an intensely Russian character throughout this movement. A sonorous percussion stroke (timpani, side and bass drums, with tam-tam) marks the start of the Allegro, a tightened, more purposeful

---

* In a strong and musical interpretation the work emerges almost convincingly. Ogan Durjan's performance with the Leipzig Gewandhaus Orchestra is most urgently recommended to those who feel disappointed by the symphony.

presentation of the above musical example now on three bassoons, with clarinets, then strings, gathering it up in a passage of mounting tension that recalls some of the more stressful moments of the Eleventh, high wind adding wrathful wild unisons. Side drum, at first strengthened by timpani, impels the music forward. Abruptly a reduction of temperature, but not of anxiety and unrest, brings a quiet presentation of a second subject in revolutionary-hymn style on celli and basses:

This is repeated and developed by violins in a passage of hope and expansion until the whole orchestra is singing of the bright future. It is ironic that the future should be evoked so strongly by music that gazes back unashamedly to the styles and shapes of the latter half of the Nineteenth century.

A jarring call again from percussion brings home to the prematurely exultant music the need for action to achieve that promised state: solo bassoon reintroduces the opening theme of the Allegro and the development section has begun. The second movement of the Eleventh Symphony is even more pointedly recalled: this is a different revolution but the same cause, and the music seems determined that, this time, all difficulties will be swept away. Detailed analysis of this exciting passage is hardly necessary, but the listener will doubtless notice the skill with which momentum is maintained as the second theme (quoted above) gradually assumes prominence, tending to steady the music whilst ominously muttering percussion holds the basic urgency in constant reserve. A noble brass chorale restates the theme of the introduction, complete with its four-fold hesitation, in augmentation, this time answered quietly by the muttering percussion. Development and recapitulation have been deftly telescoped, the music, in its anxiety to convey a message, having neither time nor patience for formal exactness.

As percussion continues its unnerving ostinato over a halting *pizzicato* figure the second movement, "Razliv," enters without a break. "Razliv" was the name of Lenin's hideout near Petrograd, a lonely place where the architect of the Revolution spent long and anxious hours planning details of the event that was to bathe his country in blood and replace one form of misery with another. Again celli and basses, *adagio*, announce a disturbed theme over which a solo horn intones a yearning melody which, when joined in a chorale by three colleagues, again recalls the above-quoted example; lower strings soon do likewise, while solo clarinet and flute join the basic temper of longing mixed with pain, anticipation mixed with fear. The brass chorale from the first movement reappears fleetingly, significantly without its attendant hesitant continuation. Solo flute, then bassoon, then clarinet, as if presenting differing views of the same misery, eloquently bring the slow movement to a close, but not before a sombre warning has been uttered by solo trombone. The listener may wish to construe this as representing Lenin's grimly resolute words of encouragement on the eve of the Revolution, but if the composer had any such definite intention in mind he did not publish it.

The third movement, "Aurora," enters timidly, again on *pizzicato* low strings, timpani holding a *pianissimo* roll that crystallises into the rhythm of a stirring but still subdued and expectant march*:

It was the battle cruiser "Aurora" that fired the first shots on the Winter Palace, impelling those inside to surrender to the Bolsheviks. The gradually increasing strength of the march flows and ebbs as timpani mutter once more under soft tam-tam strokes.† Trombones and tuba introduce a soft theme:

---

* The segment marked *a* in this example will be seen to refer back to the fourth to eighth notes of the previous example.

† On page 123 of the State Music Publishers score, issued in Moscow in 1964, a swelling bass-drum roll immediately before the trombone and tuba entry is given in error to tam-tam.

—which is a serene, if faintly sinister, version of the main *motif* of the symphony (quoted on page 130)—against increasingly apprehensive wind chords and an agitated string unison in triplets. A hard, raw climax initiated by insistent percussion announces the advent at last of the successful Revolution as the music moves imperceptibly into the Finale, "Dawn of Humanity." Although the Finale commences several bars earlier, according to the score, its first theme may be said to be a triumphant subject announced on four horns in unison:

This is presented at length with great power, emphatic drum strokes marking its progress and contributing to its stern and war-like character. An *allegretto* section enters on strings: an innocuous theme of almost dance-like gaiety, extending for many bars until a solo horn, followed by a trumpet, again brings the above-quoted example to the fore. The two elements are combined loosely in a section which seems to be progressing towards a carefree climax of joyful exultation, but we are not allowed to forget the pain and horror which gave birth to the new age. Elements from the first movement are introduced, solo timpani bringing a lamenting passage which draws attention once again to the hesitating *motif* first heard near the start of the symphony. Acknowledgement thus being made to the tragic events that have led to the "new age," the music is free to move into the final coda. It is perhaps this coda that has most acutely embarrassed commentators, drawing epithets such as "tub-thumping," "pretentious," and "empty," and it is inescapable that these criticisms are eminently justified. Did Shostakovich's skill and inspiration so completely desert him here, or are we meant to draw unfavourable conclusions? As we listen in awe to the trite repetitions and the meaningless din of percussion, are we not in danger of forgetting, or having forced out of our minds, the real qualities of the earlier part of the symphony? Here, truly, it is better to travel in hope than to arrive: did Shostakovich himself feel once again that the hopes of a great and prosperous future that had been so abundant before, during, and immediately after the 1917 Revolution had not been realised under the optimistic surface gloss of the following years? It is easy to find fault with some of Shostakovich's most overtly patriotic music, but was he really much more clever than we thought at putting forward his own viewpoint, knowing all the time that his music would be analysed with interest outside Russia? Speculation will remain; meanwhile we, at least, are free to draw our own conclusions.

Thirteenth Symphony, "Babi Yar" (1962)

Controversial even before its *première*, the Thirteenth Symphony became a landmark in Shostakovich's career. All five movements caused this controversy, but none more so than the first: "Babi Yar." The orchestral accompaniment to the words is remarkably restrained and linear, emphasis being placed unmistakably on the meaning behind those words, which are presented with a beautiful clarity. It seems that, for once discarding his purely orchestral voice, Shostakovich wanted to present his message with the unambiguous force of words, even if they were written by someone else. He shared their meaning and value with Yevtushenko. Since "Babi Yar" was already under criticism as a subversive poem before Shostakovich decided to orchestrate it, and since ultimately the choice of material rested with the composer, it is certain that his intention was to file a protest not against the government but against its policies. As the composer explained in 1968: "Soviet music is a weapon in the ideological battle. Artists cannot stand as indifferent observers in this struggle."

In the Seventh, Eighth, Ninth, Eleventh and Twelfth Symphonies Shostakovich had shown a tendency to link some of his movements, particularly welding the penultimate one to the Finale in order to give the works symphonic cohesion and dramatic continuity. So, too, in the Thirteenth, the last three of the five movements are meant to be played without a break, but in other respects the work has little in common with any of its predecessors. Although scored for voices and orchestra, its method of presenting the burden of Yevtushenko's poems bears no relation to the overtly proletarian message blazed forth with little regard for taste or subtlety in the Second and Third Symphonies, nor yet to the patriotic, if possibly ambivalent, meanings behind the wordless Eleventh and Twelfth. In short, Shostakovich had reached another crisis in symphonic development, just as he had done between the Fourth and Fifth Symphonies, but whereas that crisis of 1936 had been forced upon him by external events, the new one of 1962 was clearly the result of an inner musical conviction that his exploration of the heroic/patriotic symphony had reached its termination and perhaps even gone beyond the confines which musical values dictate. Evidently it was time for him to break with his tradition, and while he was at it Shostakovich broke also with the international symphonic tradition by producing what is to all intents a symphonic song cycle or cantata of the type pioneered by Mahler in *Das Lied von der Erde.*

The symphony is intense, concentrating sheer drama throughout its pages, and all five of the poems signal protest. The second movement is particularly biting: a scherzo entitled "Humour." Although Shostakovich's writing in this movement and elsewhere in the symphony has an untypical astringency, it remains accessible—a clear indication that he wished his music to be heard and appreciated by a wide audience.

The first movement is entitled "Babi Yar," the name by which the whole symphony is known. Hugh Ottaway has drawn attention to the fact that the opus numbers of the Twelfth and Thirteenth Symphonies are consecutive and asks a pertinent question: did the composer, in following immediately a movement called "The Dawn of Humanity" with a movement focusing on the worst evils of man's inhumanity as typified by the massacre at Babi Yar, wish his audience to draw an inescapable conclusion? The sight of the giant cliff at Babi Yar, an unmarked grave for countless thousands of Jewish refugees, drew from Yevgyeni Yevtushenko one of his most chilling and powerful poems. It is no surprise that the subject and the poem appealed to the composer, who set it in music of bitter and tragic gloom.* It was largely due to the twin barbs of Yevtushenko's accusation of the continuance of anti-Semitism today in Russia and of Shostakovich's obvious agreement and

---

* Babi Yar is the name of a deep ravine lying on the north-west outskirts of Kiev. After the Germans captured Kiev in September 1941 they settled in and around a street known as Kreshchatik, a comfortable area of theatres and hotels. This whole street was blown up by a series of mines laid beforehand by the Soviet authorities,

sympathy with this dire charge that the authorities decided, after much hesitation, to ban the work outright until the poet had changed some of the most damning passages. This he did (see the Recommended Recordings section), oddly altering one passage that dealt with the death of a Jew so that it read as the deaths of Russians, Ukrainians, *and* Jews, as if many wrongs would make a single right in the eyes of the authorities. Nevertheless, the changes were slight, and much of the force of the original, together with all the force of Shostakovich's music, remains. Embarrassed by the surviving words and by the fact that the ban on the work had not come quickly enough to prevent the music leaking to the West, the Soviets firmly and uselessly locked the stable door by banning the symphony entirely after a performance of the revised version in 1965, and for more than five years the work lay dormant in the Soviet Union while the rest of the world, eagerly, if in some bewilderment, listened to a pirated Russian recording of the original version issued on the American Everest label. Not until about 1971 was the official Soviet curtain quietly lifted to allow Russian performances of the revised version, but it seems that official suspicion about the meaning of the words exists in Russia today.

There can be no doubt about the message of the first movement as Shostakovich's strongly evocative tone-painting announces a gruesome atmosphere of despair and foreboding. Four muted horns and two muted trumpets play a grief-laden *motif* over the sepulchral tones of *pizzicato*

---

and hundreds of German officers and men were killed. Apparently as a reprisal, the German command rounded up all the Jews in the city, conveyed them to Babi Yar, and systematically machine-gunned them. It is estimated that, on September 29 and 30, 1941, some 70,000 Jewish corpses fell into the ravine. The German officer in charge of this massacre was named Topaide; he has never been brought to justice. During the rest of the German occupation of Kiev—some two years—Babi Yar became a terror camp from which few Jews, Ukrainians or Russians escaped. No one knows how many more thousands died at the hands of the blood-crazed German guards and their Ukrainian and Russian helpers. When it became clear to the occupying forces that their tenancy of the area was to be temporary owing to the advance of the Russian forces, they sought ways of destroying the evidence of their atrocities. The bodies, which had been covered by soil dynamited from the ravine sides, were dug up by prisoners, stacked in piles and burned: the prisoners who had carried out this task were then themselves shot and burned, but some were not even shot first. A factory was constructed on the camp to turn human bodies into soap, but it was never completed and its contribution to the disposal of the evidence was negligible. It did however, give the Germans an idea for a euphemism: in their records Babi Yar appears as a "building company." Attempts by the Soviets to erase the memory of Babi Yar from history at first proved disastrous. A dam was built across the end of the ravine and mud and water was pumped in. The intention was to raise the level of the land as the mud settled and the water drained away. On March 13, 1961, while Shostakovich was working on his symphony, the dam collapsed, sweeping away a tram depot, a hospital, dozens of houses, and drowning and burying hundreds of people in mud. A more permanent effort to fill in Babi Yar was started the following year, and since sound engineering principles were brought to bear on building a road and apartments on the raised level, it seems that the cursed ravine has at last been eradicated from sight, if not from memory.

celli and basses,* bass clarinet, two bassoons and double bassoon (a sinister assembly of the darkest colours of the orchestra), the atmosphere of desolation completed by the solemn tolling of a bell. The male chorus (the score calls for a complement of anything from forty to a hundred singers) proclaims in dark tones that no monument stands above the graves at Babi Yar: only the cliff towers like a rough tombstone. When the bass soloist enters he expresses in forbidding tones that he identifies himself with the Russians, Ukrainians and Jews who have died there. He goes on to describe in detail the ill-treatment, cruelty and uncaring death which has been the lot of Jews through the ages, of his experiences as a young Jewish boy in Belostok, beaten up by savage half-drunk pogrom roughs who shout, "Kill the Yids—Save Russia!" as one of their number violates his mother. A snarling, leering *motif* first heard on oboes and bassoons depicts the ugly jeers of these ruffians

and this *motif* is soon taken up with abandon and extended as the onion-and-vodka-stinking rabble warm to their inhuman sport.

A return to the opening mood brings a bass solo admonishing the Russian people for allowing those "with vile hands" to pollute the race with anti-Semitic hatred while at the same time declaring themselves (chorus, with ironic emphasis) "The Union of the Russian People." Brass and percussion respond with the snarling *motif*, building it to a curt climax. A lighter section, *allegretto*, depicts the innocence of Anne Frank, hidden in a small room away from the fragrant spring but with the comforting presence of her loved one, only to be discovered by jack-booted German soldiers. As the door is crushed, her lover whispers consolingly: "It is only the breaking of the ice." She is carried away.

---

* Shostakovich calls specifically for five-string double basses.

An orchestral climax crushes all hope and is the personification of all guilt as swirling violins storm above accusing brass.

Softly the chorus paints a desolate picture of Babi Yar, of the wind in the grass, of the trees standing as if in judgement; and the soloist recalls Russia's heroic fight against Fascism. At this point the text originally called upon the soloist to identify with every old man and every small child shot without pity in that awful place, and he becomes a "titanic silent scream." In growing tension the chorus demands that the *Internationale* shall thunder forth only when every anti-Semite is buried. The soloist, allying himself to this sentiment, accepts proudly the hate of all anti-Semites, proclaiming himself for this reason to be a true Russian. A short orchestral coda brings to an end one of the most powerfully simple of all Shostakovich's movements.

The poem and music stand as a human statement designed to enlist the sympathies of all men, especially the leaders of Russia. For Shosta-kovich the issue was to define an ideal seen to be lacking at home, in artistic terms to point to a racism that should not exist anywhere, and to say that by not being overtly against racism is covertly to be for it. It was also time to declare to all listeners that Russia's leading composer had a mind of his own and was not lacking the courage to speak it out, thereby saying in addition that all Russian people had the right to feel and think. In the Soviet regime such an action proved to be too strong.

The second movement, "Humour," is a scherzo. Earlier in his career the composer had relied a great deal on humorous effects and deft, unexpected non-sequiturs of scoring, and here he returns very much to this manner of writing to portray Humour itself as a resilient imp whom no one can imprison or kill. This movement has as much bite as any Shostakovich wrote. It is perhaps a statement of personal philosophy and self-defence. After a life-long fight to have joyful, light, humorous music re-accepted as a legitimate ingredient of symphonic structure and mood, as it had been in the Eighteenth century, Shostakovich became a stubborn exponent of humour in the world of serious music. Music should entertain, Shostakovich tells us, and "sunbeams and smiles" have an honourable place in art. Critics often seem to feel that humour is out of place in Shostakovich's or any composer's music which is intended otherwise to be serious, that banality and grotesquerie were failings and not intended effects.* Shostakovich wrote material abounding in such moments and experienced criticism for it almost every time, but now he gave his final creed, with the help of Yevtushenko's poem, in an acid-etched Scherzo.

The movement is witty, satirical and parodistic; not simply light and humorous. Humour is being stifled, seized and oppressed: the authorities try to buy Humour, to kill him, to keep him from the people, but Humour is unstoppable, uncontainable. The strong opening declaration, alternating between wind and string chords, leads to a chuckle before Humour himself enters, clad in garish colours, stamping and gesturing his defiance. The soloist tells how tsars, kings, and every ruler of the earth commanded parades but none could command Humour, how attempts to buy or to kill Humour are inevitably met by a thumb to the nose.

Attempts to execute him, to stick his severed head on a pike, find the little chap bouncing back with a teasing cry of "Here I am!" (soloists and chorus in imitation) and dancing irrepressibly to a single bass-drum and triangle accompaniment. Suddenly, caught as a political prisoner, he is marched in shabby overcoat to his execution, head bowed and submissive, but with a skip he is out of his coat and away with a carefree "Bye-bye!" Attempts to hold him in cells are met with similar disdain:

---

* Truly humorous music is notoriously difficult to bring off successfully. Much wit in music will bring an amused smile to the lips of the listener, but rare indeed is music that can elicit from the audience a spontaneous guffaw at first hearing. In his youth Shostakovich produced such pieces, and here again he comes near it.

he can walk through any wall—and any person. The final toast, amid a triumphant orchestral conclusion, is: "To Humour, a brave little man."

In third place Shostakovich has presented an extraordinarily effective picture of the grey, frugal, hopeless existence of Russia's womenfolk, touching on their shameful exploitation. The scene is a grocery store in wintertime. Opening and closing with a timeless passage for celli and basses, as if to convey the fact that conditions have been and will continue to be without hope, the central section brings a lightening of scoring by imperceptible degrees and a repetitive tapping *motif* on woodblock and castanet perhaps suggesting the clanking of tins in a shopping basket as the housewives of Russia select provisions for their families. Praises of the women tell of their contribution to the existence of the state and of their hard work. Yevtushenko sees the storekeeper trying to cheat women for mere pennies to make his ends meet. The implication is that he steals from them because they are too weak to stop him. An indignant orchestral climax censures this shameful practice, but for most of the time the music rarely rises above the whisper of the women themselves as they stand in line, shopping bags in hand, waiting to pay the dishonest shopkeeper. The poet watches, himself contributing to the shopkeeper's need to steal from the women by stealing some dumplings. Guilt is in all of us and actions form a chain. This movement is a telling indictment of the featureless greyness of everyday life in the Soviet Union today.

As the hopeless low string meditation flattens out on a bare A flat octave, timpani, tam-tam and bass drum announce the beginning of the fourth movement, "Fears." A tuba solo which would not have been out of place in the Third or Fourth Symphonies but which has here an unexpected effect of incongruity

sets an extraordinary mood of still contemplation mixed with impending doom. On the words "fears are dying in Russia," the chorus continues the atmosphere, but the soloist recalls the existence of fears in the old days (i.e. presumably before the Revolution), fears of a knock on the door, of talking unwarily to foreigners—or even to a spouse. Shostakovich accompanies this long solo with an elaborate pattern of orchestration, subdued fanfare-like figures on trumpets, flutes, clarinets and other woodwind instruments supplying essential colouring over an insecure bass-line. A change of mood, the string band tapping out a rhythm with the wood of their bows, a rhythm reinforced by pianoforte and timpani, accompanies a choral episode of growing march-like intensity telling of the fearlessness with which Russia has built a nation amid snow-storms and gone into battle against its enemies to protect what had been built, but of the people's enduring fear of talking amongst themselves. In a flash of perhaps unconscious perception, it is remarked that Russia, having now conquered internal fears (*sic*), spreads even greater fear amongst her enemies. Over an agitated viola line of semiquavers, taken up from the final clarinet notes accompanying the preceding chorus, the soloist outlines the new fears that are growing: patriotic insincerity, lies, self-congratulation, distrust, all are objects of the new fears. The semiquavers are adopted by the whole string group and a piercing climax occurs in contemplation of these new and more insidious fears. The shrill clamour is silenced by a single chime. Then, in flat contradiction of what has just been exposed, the chorus returns to its first statement: "Fears are dying in Russia." As a postscript the poet admits that he has the fear himself that his lines are being written without full force. This ambiguous remark may be taken as a self-criticism that the poet is unable to put into words the great wonder of the new fearless Russia. Alternatively, and surely more likely in view of the rest of the poem's content, it is an indication that a deathly fear of writing the truth still exists there; that the fears, far from dying, have mutated into something far more chilling, but that the state need fear nothing from its loyal subjects if only fears could really be eliminated.

"Fears" is the most elaborate of the symphony's five movements. It uses a variety of ideas and textures to stress its tense message; from angry march to soft self-doubt and violent questionings, the words come forth, one eye on the conviction of truth and the other on the agents of suppression. This poem represents a clear protest against the sup-pressive nature of the Soviet government. Second to the "Babi Yar" movement, "Fears" was most viciously attacked by the bureaucrats. To satisfy the government and keep the symphony in performance, seven lines of the poem were altered. If one reads the different versions it will be seen that references to imprisonment without trial, to neglect of the poor, and to the fear experienced by artists, have been replaced, but by hardly less contentious lines, and those last four lines of clearly expressed fear which remained in the 1965 version keep the true meaning apparent.

By comparison with the other four movements, the Finale, "A Career," is more reliant on purely orchestral passages as links between the various vocal statements. After "Fears" the movement sounds light, almost inconsequential, as two flutes embark on a carefree, rhapsodic melody, almost like the absent-minded whistling of an artisan happy with his lot and his career:

Smoothly, other woodwind accompany this idea until eventually it is taken up in similar vein by strings. Just before the entry of the solo voice, a bassoon presents a playful phrase which is to appear throughout the movement in various guises:

Soloist and chorus take it in turns to explain that the following of a true career should be a fearless undertaking, and they exemplify Galileo who, despite opposition, maintained that the Earth revolved around the Sun while a now unremembered colleague, knowing this to be true, yet denied it so that he might not risk his position or the security of his family. Other great careerists are cited: Shakespeare, Pasteur, Newton and Tolstoy. "Lev?" asks the soloist. "Lev!" confirms the chorus with a shout. Those who cursed them for their genius are forgotten while the brave pioneers will be remembered forever. Yevtushenko brings his examples up-to-date by recalling those who yearned for the stratosphere and the doctors who gave their lives in the fight against cholera; then inevitably the pertinent comparison is drawn: those artists who today speak the truth will surely be remembered while those who vilify them will as assuredly be forgotten. The laughter in the music is a mocking challenge to the state: undermine me if you will, but my career is furthered by my telling the truth and by being challenged by you for it. With great power the orchestra approaches the final lines, then subsides to allow a parting shot: "All those with careers, their faith makes me a man. Therefore I will work at my own career by doing my best *not* to work at it." Is this a jibe at the need for doing hack work to placate the patron State? A lyrical passage uniting the conviction of the two artists—poet and composer—leads to a single farewell toll of the bell, and the symphony closes on a serene note.

In this Thirteenth Symphony the composer dared the Soviet leaders to prove that he was wrong about them; instead he was shown to be right, and that fears were indeed *not* dying in Russia. Although the Thirteenth Symphony is now back in the approved repertoire inside Russia the conflicts that arose from the government's disapproval of the poetry and of the composer's sympathy with its message led to the second longest gap between symphonies in Shostakovich's career.

Fourteenth Symphony (1969)

This symphony was premiered on September 29, 1969, in Leningrad, Rudolf Barshay conducting the Moscow Chamber Orchestra with soloists Galina Vishnyevskaya, soprano, and Mark Reshetin, bass. With this work, even more so than with the Thirteenth, Shostakovich essentially declared the symphonic form a free agent, answering the perennial question, "What is a symphony?" with: whatever the composer wishes it to be as long as the result is satisfactory.

The music of the Fourteenth is Shostakovich at his most sombre, and no laughter or gaiety will be found in its pages, except the ironic laughter of a bitter woman. In comparison with earlier works the composer has penetrated a totally different sphere. In 1966 he had almost died from a heart attack. He never fully recovered and his last nine years were filled with illness, another heart attack finally killing him in August 1975. Confronted by his own mortality in such an immediate and direct manner, Shostakovich in his Fourteenth Symphony gave us a statement about what he saw and felt in death. He does not look at death philosophically, but poetically and mundanely. His intention seems to be to state the human view of death: the ugly, grim aspects that the prospect of dying presents to the human being not yet willing to die. We are to conclude that Death is always there, waiting, and we must cope with this fact and take it into consideration constantly. The composer does not say how or why we must consider; he merely finds himself considering. The symphony is deeply religious in its way, profoundly moving and tightly presented despite the apparently elaborate size of its canvas. In fact it is one of Shostakovich's most restrained works, using an economy of orchestration to create a diversity of effect. The score presents a human thanatopsis—looking at Death starkly and directly, as did Tchaikovsky in his Sixth Symphony and, on a much wider scale, perhaps Vaughan Williams in the final movement of *his* Sixth Symphony. It is at times chilling, occasionally comforting, often frightening, but in many respects purely beautiful. "Shostakovich has surfaced with one of the most profoundly personal scores he has ever written. I will go further: this symphony is likely to find a place among the most enduring creations" (Peter Heyworth, writing in the "New York Times").

The Fourteenth Symphony, in eleven movements, is unorthodox from first to last and is unique in the symphonic repertoire. It is certainly far from the Soviet ideal of heroic realism in music. Instead it is tragic and subjective, its format and content inviting criticism from the Soviet government; yet criticism did not come. The work was immediately and unanimously acclaimed. Once again Shostakovich had not yielded, but had maintained his own credo that the end justifies the means in music as long as the means selected serve the end intended. It was the Soviet government's turn to yield. Was this because Shostakovich had become too feted to be criticised, or because the leaders of the Soviet Union wanted to present to the West an image of free expression, even though Solzhenitsyn came under attack for "Gulag Archipelago" and Kuznetsov had elected to defect? Perhaps, as in the case of his Fifth Symphony, Shostakovich had written a score too powerfully effective to be criticised. In any case, the music won its own support, at least among the public. The complicated, loaded, dissonant, restrained symphony was simple in approach and easily accessible despite its often uncomfortably "modern" language. Even so, its messages are deep and its laconic orchestration places high demands upon the listener's attention. In the West the work met with similar success, proving that its messages have universal relevance.

The Fourteenth Symphony is scored for soprano and bass voices with a chamber (one is almost tempted to say "skeleton") orchestra of strings and percussion. In his handling of the string group the composer looked back to the Second and Fifth Symphonies: violins are frequently divided, once extending to as many as ten different voices and, as in the Thirteenth Symphony, five-string double basses are required. In the percussion department are to be found castanets, wood block, whip, chimes, vibraphone, xylophone, celesta, and tom-toms in soprano, alto and tenor ranges.* The plan of the music revolves around eleven poems about death by four poets: two by Federico García Lorca (Spanish; died during the Spanish Civil War in 1936); six by Apollinaire (French, 1880–1918); one by Wilhelm Karlovich Küchelbecker (a close friend of Pushkin and a political exile after the abortive 1825 Decembrist revolt against Tsar Nikolay I); and two by Rainer Maria Rilke (German philosopher/poet, who formed many of his religious beliefs upon visiting Russia in 1899 and again in 1900, giving particular poetic expression to the belief that God is present in all things; died of blood poisoning in 1926). Even the choice of poems invites controversy: only one is by a Russian, and the choice of two by a German religious philosopher such as Rilke to close the work must have been a hard pill for the Soviet government to swallow. Shostakovich's boldness must be admired.

I: "De Profundis," by García Lorca, is a miniature of amazing restraint and economy. Percussion is held in reserve, the dynamic level does not rise above *piano*, and the bass soloist is dovetailed with an undulating violin line

that suggests the desolate scene at a red sand graveyard in Córdoba in which are buried "a hundred fervent lovers." This is the sombre loneliness of Death, etched in an unchanging *adagio* tempo.

II: "Malagueña" (*allegretto*), also by García Lorca, is a violent contrast, even though percussion is still withheld until the entry of castanets six bars from the end. Violins play the hectic Spanish dance in rapid figurations as the soprano tells of Death stalking a tavern even as the merrymakers drink and sing. Death strides in and out as chairs are overturned in an effort to escape. This is a picture of Death the grotesque and obscene: "Black horses and black souls lurk inside the

---

* The Fourteenth is the only one of Shostakovich's symphonies to omit timpani.

guitar; the stink of salt and hot blood invades the blooms of the nervous sea."

III: "Lorelei," by Apollinaire. For the most part this long poem is set at a hurtling *allegro molto* in dialogue mixed with narrative. Lorelei was the sad beauty whose irresistible attraction for men led to her being condemned to life in a convent in the absence of her loved one. The Bishop orders three knights to take her thence but on the way she tricks them and throws herself into the Rhein as her beloved approaches in a boat. Here, Death comes as a friend to a desperate maiden, and the music ideally depicts that desperation and the yearning for her lover, xylophone and wood block contributing to the distraught mood. When the knights march poor Lorelei to the convent the composer introduces a ruthless march, and celesta portrays the girl's reflection as she gazes for the last time into the Rhein. Two chimes bring an *adagio* passage as she sees her beloved's boat on the river below. With notable restraint Shostakovich allows the Bishop to tell of her sudden plunge into the water, gravely describing the colour of her eyes and hair in the depths. Vibraphone ripples as her body sinks, and a solo cello sings a requiem.

IV: "The Suicide" (*adagio*) by Apollinaire follows appropriately, a continuation of the cello's lonely line confirming the connection. Of almost unearthly beauty, the movement opens with the soprano singing of the three lilies that alone mark the suicide's grave:

Rich harmonies portray the majestic beauty of the lilies as they stand defiant against rain from a black sky. Nobility and beauty turn to horror as one lily, growing from the fatal wound, glows blood-red in the sunset. The opening strain returns with clouded beauty. Anguished music tells of the second lily, drawing its nourishment from a broken and worm-eaten heart, while the roots of the third lily probe and lacerate the maiden's mouth. The beauty of the lilies is, like her life, cursed. The final appearance of the "three lilies" *motif* is accompanied by a solo double bass as the movement ends in deepest despair.

V: "Waiting I," by Apollinaire. A young soldier, too young to have experienced the joys of love, waits bravely for the enemy in a trench. His sister has a premonition that he is to die before nightfall: she sacrifices herself in incestuous love for his sake. Shostakovich sets the military scene with a xylophone *motif* rhythmically akin to the fanfare that announced the Finale of the Eleventh Sympathy. Then, one player in charge of all three tom-toms accompanies the pitying girl's solo. Rich *glissandi* and varied percussion point a sardonic mood parodying a military march.

VI: "Waiting II" (also called: "Madame, Look!") by Apollinaire, is a short but biting Adagio. Death has broken madame's heart and in defence she laughs at her dead lover. The word "laugh" (the harsh, rhythmic *khokhocho*) dominates the movement with searing bitterness. Only Death can reunite the lovers.

VII: "In Prison," by Apollinaire. A remarkable evocation of the living death of solitary imprisonment, the poem is akin to the powerful writing of Solzhenitsyn when describing his own incarceration in prison camps. "Here I am dead to everyone," laments Apollinaire. The poet spent several days in prison, falsely accused of an art theft, and he remained a prisoner until cleared. He sensed a certain death there. The prisoner cries to the Almighty for pity and for the preservation of his reason. As evening falls he finds comfort in the fact that he is no longer alone in his cell: a single light above his head keeps him company, and he equates this light with his own mind. The central section of this black picture of hopelessness portrays the deep timeless silence of imprisonment, strings, *col legno*, and wood block marking the interminable minutes and hours with an even, plodding rhythm.

VIII: "Answer of the Zaporozhian Cossacks to the Sultan of Constantinople." The last of Apollinaire's poems is a bitter and acid attack on a symbol of pure evil, born when the sultan's mother writhed in spasms of filth. Which sultan this refers to is unclear, but the reference takes place during the Russo-Turkish War of 1769–74. The sultan offered the choice of death or clemency, but the latter only if the Cossacks switched allegiance. The Cossacks refused the choice of a tainted life, just as Shostakovich himself refused to lower his standards for the sake of Soviet realism. Death is not singled out here, but, through implication, butchery is. The music reflects the invective of the words and, towards the end, the violins divide into ten shivering, polytonal voices as the

Cossacks, having delivered their fearless and vituperative answer, are ruthlessly executed.

IX: "O Delvig, Delvig" (*andante*) by Küchelbecker, is the only Russian poem in the cycle. The setting simply states the hope that the art of one's life-long creative efforts will survive Death and thus bestow immortality. Küchelbecker, exiled to Siberia, says in this poem that deeds and songs will forever be remembered and this makes tyrants tremble. Art is the only true monument no matter what men in power might try to do to it and to its creators. This is a direct message to all artists everywhere, filled with both joy and sorrow. If deeds have lasted beyond the lifetime of their creator, then after all the creator endures. Percussion is silent here, and the string band is pared down to intimate proportions in a movement that reduces Death to a matter of little importance amid the continuing affairs of man.

In the last two poems, both by Rilke, the composer has selected texts which possibly have strong personal relevance.

X: "The Death of a Poet" (*largo*). The opening of the symphony is recalled (see page 145) as the soprano once again conveys loneliness and distance by using the high register of her voice. To Rilke's mystical text she sings that the poet is dead, that the life mask of his face has turned to pale indifference. The dead poet no longer cares about the living world and has instead put on his death mask, leaving us alone. The saddest part is that each of us wears a life mask that is doomed some day to decay to that same lonely indifference. The scoring is quietly tormented.

XI: Conclusion: "Almighty Death" (*moderato*), based on lines by Rilke, begins on a soft castanet and wood-block stroke, then strings, alternately *pizzicato* and *col legno*, as the two soloists in unison proclaim the bitter coda: "Almighty Death, on watch even in our happiest hours. At the peak of life it watches and waits, lives and thinks and weeps within us." A brief, hard, juddering string passage of ever-decreasing note values and ever-increasing volume brings this despairing symphony to an end:

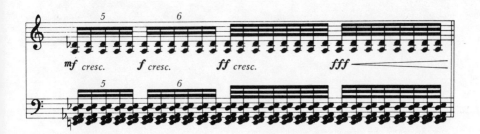

Many listeners may not wish to be bothered by contemplations of Death, but we all have pondered upon the subject at one time or another: its unfairness; the vision of the tomb; aspects apart from religion and even aspects that religion sometimes cannot comfort. If you find yourself troubled, Shostakovich is sharing your fears and hoping that by sharing he can help, but, in what may prove to be a Twentieth-century master-piece, the composer gives no answers.

The symphony was dedicated to another brilliant artist of deep talent who has since been claimed, all too soon, by Death: the English composer/conductor Benjamin Britten, whom Shostakovich once com-plimented for his outer simplicity and inner depth of emotional effect. On June 14, 1970, Britten conducted the English Chamber Orchestra at the Aldeburgh Festival in the Western *première* of the work. When the performance was over, Britten picked up the score and kissed it. The Fourteenth Symphony forms a bridge between life and death, between total abandon and the often inaccessible philosophical level of confronta-tion with the spectre of dying. If Dmitri Shostakovich is to be remembered for only one work, this symphony may well be that work.

Fifteenth Symphony (1971)

Shostakovich announced no programme for this work, his first "absolute" symphony since the Tenth, written eighteen years earlier, but as was so often the case with this composer's non-programmatic scores, a programme was sought. Maxim Shostakovich, the composer's son, provided only one clue when he revealed that his father had indicated that the first movement represented a toy store, but he did not elucidate further. Maxim stated: "The Fifteenth moves through many changes of mind. Personally, I feel it reflects the great philosophical problems of a man's life cycle, from the appearance of certain childish emotions to the acquisition of energy, vitality and wisdom. In the Finale the storms subside and there emerges triumphant a sincere feeling of humanity and great philosophical peace. But as I say, this is my personal feeling." What is significant is that this is the last symphony composed by a man very much aware of his own mortality at the time. Shostakovich looks back, quoting his own music and that of others to build his thematic ideas, and he also remembers his playfulness and penchant for laughter. Even so, the score seems to be rather a transitional work than a definitive symbolic statement for the world. Perhaps it is the

Fourteenth Symphony that stands as a better choice for the grand summation of Shostakovich's philosophy at the end of an active and troubled life. The Fifteenth represents life in retrospect, but not life that is over. The feeling that comes out of the Finale is that even though Death approaches there will be more activity in whatever time remains. One might be tempted to say much more about a composer's last symphony, but perhaps too much has already been said. It seems certain that Shostakovich meant his Fifteenth Symphony to be taken in the same vein as the Sixth and Ninth: as pure music.

There is a sparseness in the orchestration, a fascination with chamber sonorities (the full orchestra is used in only thirty-one bars throughout the work), and a further fascination with the variety and *timbres* of small percussion instruments, an interest shared by a number of other Twentieth-century composers: Hindemith, Havergal Brian, Vaughan Williams and Carl Orff come to mind, and it is perhaps significant that the two Englishmen of this group turned increasingly to percussion effects as they grew older, just as did Shostakovich. The Russian included in his score, in addition to timpani, bass drum and side drum (tamburo militare), the following percussion instruments: triangle, castanets, soprano tom-tom, wood block, whip, cymbals, tam-tam, xylophone, chimes, vibraphone and celesta, thereby extending by the "Turkish instruments" (triangle and cymbals) even the large complement required for the Fourteenth Symphony. In addition to strings the orchestra consists of piccolo, two each of flutes, oboes, clarinets, bassoons and trumpets, four horns, three trombones and tuba. Apart from the enlarged percussion department, the scoring requirement is, in fact, smaller by one trumpet than that of the First Symphony. Comparison of the two scores is instructive in other ways, too. The vast world of experience of the intervening forty-five years shows graphically in the way the composer has pared down his requirements and maximised the potential of each instrument; in short, how he required of each player much more economy of effort, just as a great poet can convey more in fifty words than can a promising one in five hundred.

After constant experiment with the number of movements an ideal symphony should have, in his last statement Shostakovich returns to the time-honoured number of four, and furthermore the order of the movements (fast/ slow/ scherzo/ fast) is even more traditional than his more usual succession, which often reversed the central two. The Largo and Scherzo are here connected. Although the main tempo of both outer movements is *allegretto*, the basic pulse may still be described as "fast," even when, as at the very end of the work, it is only the percussive effects that are maintaining the motion.

The first movement opens with a familiar formula, the rhythmic drive, melodic shape and disposition of voices being inescapably that of

Shostakovich. After two chimes on a high E, the first subject is announced:

Few more innocuous themes occur in modern symphonic music. Against light encouragement from strings and bells, the flute continues merrily, the bassoon eventually taking up the same mood, and as other instruments join the happy gallop the trumpet enters with its own version:

Almost inevitably this leads to a passage that has had commentators digging furiously for some inner meaning: a simple, straightforward presentation of the gallop *motif* from Rossini's *Guillaume Tell* Overture, acknowledged immediately by xylophone and giggling strings, and eventually leading to a cadence with comically out-of-synchronisation timpani. A side-drum roll, a trumpet fanfare, and much play from tom-tom, bells, xylophone and piccolo shows that we are truly in a toy store, and in the model soldier department at that. Is Shostakovich telling us that war is a game to be played only by immature minds? Perhaps for once we should avoid crediting the composer with inner meanings and appreciate for its own sake the vitality and variety of the music, wondering in passing just why he decided to include a most ugly bitonal horn *glissando*, why the giggling string figure should be transferred menacingly to low strings, then to all the strings, then wind, in furious conflict, at the height of which the toy trumpet once again recalls his Rossini tune, and why the hints of darker things should be swept away so completely as solo violin takes up the opening theme. In a passage which reverses the "stationary accelerando" technique of the opening of the Second Symphony, first violins moving in even quavers are joined by seconds and violas in crotchet triplets, then by celli and basses in slower five-time. Is Shostakovich telling us now that the momentum he has built up is too fast for his true message to emerge and it must therefore be slowed down gradually? Evidently not, since the irrepressible trumpet leads the music, via a climax, back to its original mood and a teasing triplet figure on various small percussion instruments sets off the solo violin a-giggling uncontrollably. The tone of the rest of the movement is set. The "slowing down" idea is transferred to woodwind, clarinets have their go at the *Guillaume Tell* fragment, and the timpanist is *still* unable to finish with the rest of the orchestra.

If any construction is to be put on the music, so like the first movement of the Ninth Symphony in its carefree gaiety, it must surely be the joy of living that may yet be experienced by a man so full of years. Those years brought with them also an absolute mastery over the orchestra. As a single example we may cite the "slowing down" idea. In the "stationary accelerando" at the start of the Second Symphony the effect is more striking on paper than in performance, whereas the "stationary ritardando" in the Fifteenth is more successful heard than read in the score. Here is experience in action—the young composer could not have known how his effect would sound when he first conceived it, but the old man was fully aware of the effect that would be produced, and by telescoping the instrumental entries he reduced the time scale of the sequence and therefore maximised its impact.

Opening with a sombre brass chorale reminiscent of a number of earlier examples, and continuing with a cello solo which recalls some of the most elegiac writing of the late string quartets, the Adagio has a sublime simplicity. These two elements alternate, expanding their reach little by little, woodwind, then muted horn, chords answering the cello's last statement. Over a trilling solo cello and low string *pizzicato* accompaniment, flutes chant in sad sixths. A trombone solo then takes up the flutes' chant at a slightly faster pace (*largo*) as tuba provides a sonorous and slow-moving accompaniment over *pizzicato* double bass, and flutes and muted trumpet join the threnody, solo violin bringing a strident climax. Wood block, in the funereal rhythm of the flutes' first melody, leads to a return to *adagio* tempo as celesta and vibraphone bring a sombre coda, the rhythm fading out on timpani; but the last sounds that are heard in this movement are three unexpected rasping bassoon chords, each *ff diminuendo*, which shatter the mood of mourning in favour of something grotesque and satirical.

Solo clarinet, prancing like some deformed hobgoblin, is greeted by piccolo and flutes in a shriek. In effect and even in instrumentation the passage is startlingly like the first entry of the *idée fixe* in the Finale of Berlioz's *Symphonie fantastique*. Solo violin, used by Saint-Saëns, Tartini, Stravinsky and others to portray the Devil, then takes up the tune, if "tune" is not too exalted a word for it. The movement gets under way amid orchestration as bright as any in earlier symphonies, driven gently but persistently by tom-tom, until a *glissando* trombone perhaps signifies its boredom with the meaningless prattle—as a similar instrument at a similar point in the "Humoreske" of Nielsen's Sixth Symphony also signalled its disgust at musical time-killing. Celli and basses dance in ungainly fashion as glittering percussion recall the delicate rhythmic end of the Scherzo of Shostakovich's own Fourth Symphony. To bring a touch of sanity to the music the violins try to establish a sober version of the continuation of the opening theme, but it seems doomed from the start and slips ever lower. Finally, the violins let it go with an irritable gesture:

Amid music that runs the constant risk of disintegrating, sparkling percussion is the only unifying factor as the movement, as if exhausted, draws to a soft conclusion.

Even in a symphony that has already drawn heavily on earlier ideas by Shostakovich himself and by other composers, it is yet a shock to encounter the Fate *motif* from Wagner's *Die Walküre* in the *adagio* introduction to the Finale, the more so since it stands cold and forbidding before one of the friendliest themes that Shostakovich ever wrote, a melody of such sweetness and insouciance that once again we are tempted to seek some explanation, draw some extra-musical meaning from the music:

At length a *staccato* brass passage, quiet and mysterious, brings a new idea: a duet for flute and oboe, then oboe and clarinet, flowing over to violins before giving way to a playful idea (oboe echoed by bassoon) which darkens as timpani adopt its rhythm. The Fate *motif* reappears and immediately the celli and basses announce the beginning of a bass-line which is to form the foundation of a passacaglia of growing intensity. This bass-line is evidently meant to recall the characteristic rhythm that underpinned the whole of the central section of the first movement of the "Leningrad Symphony." The climax is approached with inexorable power amid melodic fragments and rhythms that recall, as if in a dream, the nightmare of the Leningrad siege nearly thirty years earlier. Trumpets and trombones blaze out the rhythm at the height of the movement in a boldly impassioned Adagio. Under side-drum and tam-tam accompaniment the low strings suggest the tragic aftermath of that battle, and two bassoons with spasmodic comments from violas and celli—and a substantial interruption from clarinet with the evident intention of lightening the mood by the reintroduction of its playful *motif*—bring yet again Wagner's noble sequence. Muted horns link it unmistakably with the chorale sections of the slow movement, returning like a haunted memory from the past. Small percussion make a new appearance as quiet warning chords interrupt the melody, and the brass once again refer forbiddingly to the "Leningrad" rhythm. Celesta climbs gracefully with a nod towards the opening movement's first subject, and the way is clear at last for a long conclusion of shimmering percussion over an interminable chord which would be a clear, sunlit, A major were it not for the absence of the essential C sharp. Percussion fades away, as does the chord. Are we to be left in the air with an incomplete harmony? As a last gesture of consolation, celesta, bells and triangle supply a beautifully rich and full three-octave C sharp. Shostakovich's symphonic statement is complete.

Epilogue

About a year before his death it was reported in the West that Shostakovich had begun work on a Sixteenth Symphony. Two movements, we were told, had been completed; the rest was still in the composer's head. Further details about the style, mood and character of the work were not forthcoming, and no word has yet been received from the Soviet Union that Shostakovich's "Unfinished Symphony" is to be published there. We are free to speculate, idly and uselessly, but perhaps entertainingly, upon what a new symphony might have contained. After the Fourteenth, which dealt so decisively with Death in its many guises, admirers could hardly imagine what would be left in the gamut of symphonic possibility for Shostakovich to draw on. Clearly he was not the sort of composer to take up atonalism on a large scale, yet who would have thought, after the long succession of purely orchestral symphonies from 1936 to 1961, that he would turn to cantata and song cycle for inspiration? When it came, the Thirteenth mystified listeners, and although of almost revolutionary design, the Fourteenth was less of a shock because of the precedent created by the Thirteenth. Much more mystifying was the Fifteenth at first. Some regarded it as a work of doubtful value, simplistic, naïve, and concerned with empty effects—and what should one think about those two very odd references to Nineteenth-century operatic composers? Now it has taken its place as a retrospective statement, a round-up of a number of diverse styles and ideas in his own music, unifying elements from the Fourth and Seventh Symphonies and the Second Cello Concerto, and even from some of the string quartets. The only thing not immediately apparent to the listener is the composer's musical signature DSCH (D, E flat, C, B), and even that will reveal itself in disguised form to the score-reader determined to hunt it out.* The Fifteenth Symphony may be a transitional work, but it forms a transition to what? If any part of the Sixteenth is vouchsafed to the world, we may well be in for yet another surprise.

---

* See the third movement, bars 102–105, where the *motif* appears on first and third horns transposed to B flat, B, A flat, G.

Conclusion

The symphonic form was the focal point in the art of music for the wishes and concern of the Soviet government. That government had a specific goal in mind for music in Russia: to create hopeful, spirited music—proletarian music—built on Russian themes and folk heritage, inspired by the economic successes of the state and appealing to as many people as possible. All aspects of the arts were affected by this viewpoint, generally labelled Soviet realism. In music every composer in Russia was required to concentrate his life's work on the task of providing such material. For most of these composers this created a dilemma, best summarised by Sergey Prokofiev, who honestly sought to write one form of music for the masses and one for posterity. For Shostakovich the task was simpler. He tried to build both into one, seeing this as his artistic duty. Rather than write down to the level of the majority, Shostakovich strove to bring that level higher.

The conflict, however, between artists and state was inevitable when the state began to formulate a plan for the type of music with greatest mass appeal. The leaders of Soviet Russia decided that within the structure of the symphony the most impressive and inspiring proletarian music could be presented. The Soviet symphony had to be heroic, strong, celebrant, loud, tuneful and triumphant. The form that the state envisaged was confining and unimaginative, but would serve its purpose well enough. Shostakovich, the first truly Soviet composer, would seem the ideal leader of such a movement. Both his Second and Third Symphonies had choral endings built on revolutionary themes, but the music was far from simple and certainly not tuneful. As a matter of fact, few symphonies appeared at all during the period in which the state defined its wants, and few of those were heroic in scope. Those that were have long been forgotten.

Disappointment over the lack of such scores prompted the government to turn away from the symphony to the point of abandoning the form entirely and promoting patriotic cantatas and ballets. If a new symphony appeared it was not discouraged, but the emphasis had shifted. By now it was 1936 and everyone stepped softly. Everyone, that is, except Shostakovich, who sought to regain favour by presenting a symphony. The Fifth Symphony was not the Soviet Heroic Symphony, but it was a masterpiece that no one could ignore. Shostakovich won a popular following and at the same time, by not writing what the state wanted, he probably saved the symphony in Russia. Seeing the response in Russia and throughout the world, the state again began to encourage symphonies, from 1937 onwards along looser lines. Since then the symphony has become the most popular large orchestral art-form employed by Russian composers, carrying on a tradition of the past sixty years. Russian composers have always liked the symphony as the most elaborate expression of classical music; Russian audiences have always shared that enthusiasm.

Twenty years later, in 1957, Shostakovich was inspired to make a present to Russia of a heroic symphony that almost redefined the Soviet heroic concept. The score worked because it was still the composer's creation and desire: the Eleventh Symphony demonstrated what the state had always wanted but rarely got. However, when Shostakovich tried to explore the format further in his Twelfth Symphony, the effort fell flat, not because the music itself was of low quality (except in the Finale) but because it seemed to try too hard to protest the triumph of Soviet thought. He turned instead to a new sense of drama in his Thirteenth Symphony, again enhancing the symphonic form.

*

Categorising Twentieth-century composers in his book "What to Listen for in Music," Aaron Copland listed Shostakovich as "easily accessible." In a short phrase one composer accurately labelled another and pointed to Shostakovich's main significance as a composer. For, among composers who wrote in this century, Shostakovich *is* accessible. That is not to say that his ideas and contexts are simple: his canvases are complex and many of his ideas are strange at first. But it is for his accessibility that Shostakovich will remain important.

His conservative voice was not overly innovative in style, though he was highly creative within and around the symphonic form. Despite his conservatism, in terms of orchestration and musical ideas he was among the most original of his time: though he encouraged experimentation in others his own experimentation was limted; he solidified rather than revolutionised. Like a second-generation revolutionary he often sorted the seeming good from the seeming bad and tried every road to prove that the Revolution itself was not merely destructive but creative and continuative. He was never comfortable if his ideas led him to extreme measures: he would examine them and quickly return to a more conventional path. His music was not abstract though it contained many abstract ideas and was driven by modern energy and nervousness.

The music penned by Shostakovich shares several common aspects. It is almost always vibrant, energetic and *nervous;* often it is gay, robust and youthful. In contrast, his introspective pages bear the stamp of tragedy. Shostakovich, even in his deepest, most contemplative moods, designed his material to help celebrate life. There are moments in Shostakovich that seem thick or theatrical, old, dated, or standard, but these are few and usually—from the composer's standpoint—to good purpose. They can be very effective, even stirring, or funny. Shostakovich has been accused of banality both at home and abroad, while spending much of his time defending what others called banal and showing a place for it in serious music—his sense of humour demanded expression. Shostakovich has also been accused of a lack of self-criticism—and he was a quick worker who hated to re-write—but revision, self-criticism and formulation went on before note hit paper.

Beethoven was his model. He considered Beethoven the only true forerunner of the revolutionary movement. From his master Shostakovich drew the image of man the reasoning democrat as the centre of the universe, and the concept of victory through struggle. From Tchaikovsky he drew much of his sense of Russian music and a feeling for melody. Tchaikovsky also demonstrated for him tense emotion and the desire to understand man in pain and in sorrow. From Glazunov, his teacher, and through him from Rimsky-Korsakov, Shostakovich derived his sense of Russian folk heritage and Russian nationalism. From Gustav Mahler Shostakovich received the idea of the value of the symphonic form and the nature of orchestratien. Mahler also gave him the value, feeling and flair for sarcasm in serious music. In himself Shostakovich found the need to make his audiences smile with humour and beauty. He also had the need to reach as many people as possible, to have a rapport with his audience. Finally, as to the purpose of a Soviet artist, he said, "Good music lifts and heartens people for work and effort. It may be tragic but it must be strong."

One other factor entered into his nature. Shostakovich's artistic ego caused him more than once in his youth to feel that he was the successor to Beethoven. When he became exposed to Mahler he encountered symphonies on such a large scale that his natural talent led him to believe he could excel Mahler too. More than once he was given to grandiose ideas but with maturity came restraint. Though his music was often long and difficult, it became less and less pretentious.

The hero of his works was at times the Russian people, at times the revolutionaries who brought good changes, at times Shostakovich himself as a symbol of the people or a voice of their sufferings and joys. Sometimes the hero was the composer himself as the lone suffering artist. Never was the hero the Soviet state; it was always Man, as Shostakovich felt him through immediate experience. Even in his wartime symphonies Shostakovich did not pay tribute to the victorious or struggling state but rather to the people behind the state, the people of Leningrad or the Red Army or peasants in the war effort.

Dmitri Shostakovich believed in his homeland and was proud to be a Russian, and he attempted all his life to develop in Russia a sense of art for art's sake that would not be incompatible with Soviet realism. He knew that true art did not have to come literally from the soil, from folk songs and factories; he knew that true art was not to be found by committee or contrivance. Shostakovich always believed he had found the middle ground, the solution, by creating powerful, sometimes playful music of wide appeal and sophisticated origins.

It can be quickly pointed out—as almost every obituary tried to—that Shostakovich seems to have no successors of world prominence. Russian composers after Prokofiev, Myaskovsky and Shostakovich that have been heard in the West are unimpressive at best, the exceptions being Herman Galynin, who died in 1966, Rodion Shchedrin, who is largely given to traditional forms, and Moysey Vaynberg, whose original ideas in traditional moulds may point the way to the future of Russian symphonies. But our pessimism remains and, if justified—we must hope it is not—then excellence in concert music in Russia may have died with the composer who spent his lifetime fighting to preserve and enhance it. Only time will tell if the death of Shostakovich portends a musical tragedy.

Appendix

Further Reading

Unfortunately, most biographies of Shostakovich lie on library shelves, dated and biased. Their information is valuable but their slant is decidedly geared towards not offending the Soviet government, and none of them covers Shostakovich's mature period. D. Rabinovich's "Dmitri Shostakovich Composer" (Foreign Language Publisher Institute, Moscow, 1959) covers the most material, taking us from the First Symphony through to the Eleventh. It is markedly Soviet in viewpoint and tends to explain away any aspect of Shostakovich's work that does not strictly comply with Soviet limitations. Victor I. Seroff's "Dmitri Shostakovich—The Life and Background of a Soviet Composer" (Books for Library Press, Freeport, New York, 1943) was chiefly prompted by the sensational success of the "Leningrad Symphony." It is by far the most entertaining book on the composer and relates a great many details of his growing up and his family tree. It makes fascinating reading though it stops when Shostakovich is thirty-six. Ivan Martinov's "Shostakovich: The Man and His Work" (Philosophical Library, New York, 1946) is Shostakovich's official biography. This lends a certain credence to the words, and Martinov gives free interpretations to Shostakovich the man and Shostakovich the symphonist. Martinov's impressions are invaluable. Though, strictly speaking, he is still attached to a Soviet guideline for interpretation, he goes out on a limb more than once in defence of his subject. His one drawback is a penchant for finding programmatic reference points for everything.

Norman V. Kay's "Shostakovich" (Oxford University Press, London, 1971) is the most up-to-date writing. However, it is a limited source because its author concentrates on a few works for interpretation in order to defend Shostakovich's importance to modern music. It is an admirable defence.

For a quick, capsule introduction to Shostakovich, or for that matter to almost any other significant composer in the last three hundred years, pick up David Ewen's "Musical Masterworks." It is entertaining and informative, although decidedly limited by the sheer vastness of the ground it tries to cover. For a strongly written book that covers Soviet music, there is no better source than Boris Schwarz's "Music and Musical Life in Soviet Russia" (Barrie and Jenkins, London, 1972). The book is an all-inclusive look at how Soviet composers tried to handle the struggle for expressive freedom against a suppressive Soviet regime, how they fared and what they did to comply with Soviet wishes. Shostakovich figures prominently in the book, indicating his importance, and Schwarz traces Shostakovich's musical and political development with vigour and keen interest.

Alexander Werth's "Musical Uproar in Moscow" (Turnstile Press, London, 1949) is a short but concise version of the 1948 Zhdanov Decree and its effects, well worth reading if you are interested in that monumental sham. Werth also gives the definitive source on "Russia at War" (E. P. Dutton, New York, 1964) that, along with Harrison E. Salisbury's "900 Days: The Siege of Leningrad" (Harper and Row, New York, and Secker and Warburg, London, 1969), should provide enough information about the Russian wartime experience. An even better source is Kuznetsov's "Babi Yar, A Document in the Form of a Novel" (Farrar, Straus and Giroux, and Simon and Schuster, New York, 1970; originally published by Yunost in the U.S.S.R. in 1966, censored version). "Babi Yar" relates a boy's exposure to the occupation of the Ukraine by the Germans and German treatment of Jews, Russians and Ukrainians (in that order) at infamous Babi Yar. For curiosity one might also look at John Toland's "The Last 100 Days" (Random House, New York, 1965) and Kurt Vonnegut Jr.'s brilliant novel "Slaughterhouse Five" (Dell Publishing Co., New York, 1969) for accounts of the fire-bombing of Dresden that so impressed Shostakovich in 1960. And no Shostakovich-lover's bookshelf is complete without the slim volume, "Dmitri Shostakovich—A Complete Catalogue," compiled by Malcolm MacDonald (Boosey & Hawkes, London, 1977), a non-thematic chronological listing with useful indices.

Finally, a good history of the Russian nation from birth to today is George Vernadsky's "A History of Russia" (Yale University Press, New Haven, Conn., 1929, and Bantam Books, New York, 1967). This very readable account provides background on the entire Russian experience.

Recommended Recordings

The following list of recommended recordings of Shostakovich's symphonies does not take into account the current availability of performances since, in these days of frequent re-issues, one never knows when an old recording of a high-quality performance will reappear on the market. Inclusion in this list is dependent upon the performance reaching a high level of technical achievement, the reading being stylish and authentic, and the recording being of reasonably faithful quality. *In no way is this list intended to be an exhaustive discography.* Subjective impressions of these performances are included to amplify the information, and facts concerning presentation are given where necessary. Couplings of other Shostakovich works are also shown. Where a recording has been on the market more than once, only the maker's latest known number is given. The first disc number is for the U.K. issue; the American record number is always prefixed by "US." Mono-only records are identified by (M), and, where issues were made in both mono and stereo, only the numbers for the latter pressings are given. At the time of writing, only one issue has been made in simulated stereo: Toscanini's coupling of the First and Seventh Symphonies.

It is possible to give a blanket recommendation to the British Melodiya/HMV thirteen-disc set (not available in this format in America) of all the symphonies in Russian performances (HMV SLS 5025) despite some criticisms of a few of the performances. The recordings therein are listed separately below with artists' details and with separate record numbers; short comments are added to indicate the nature of artistic or recording reservations.

No. 1 in F minor, op. 10 (1925)

Ančerl—Czech Philharmonic Orchestra.
    (*Festive Overture*) Supraphon SUAST 50576; US: Artia S 710.
Horvat—Zagreb Philharmonic Orchestra.
    (Symphony No. 9) Turnabout TV 34223.
Kondrashin—Moscow Philharmonic Orchestra.
    (in complete set) HMV SLS 5025; (Symphony No. 3) HMV ASD 3045;
    (Symphony No. 2) US: Angel S 40236.

Ormandy—Philadelphia Orchestra.
(Cello Concerto No. 1) CBS 72081; US: Columbia MS 6124.
Toscanini—NBC Symphony Orchestra.
(Symphony No. 7) RCA Victrola VICS 6038.

Ančerl's performance is recommendable for fine orchestral playing and a good grasp of the music, but his slack, almost maudlin, approach to the slower sections may deter some listeners. Kondrashin's fluid account realises much of the young composer's daring originality in excellent recorded sound. He brings out unexpected depth in the first movement which helps the work to adhere more successfully than in some more brilliant performances. Ormandy's is a hard-hitting and finely disciplined performance strongly realising the stature of the music. Despite its age (it was first issued in 1960) the recording still sounds excellent. Much older (March 12, 1944) but more than adequate in its electronic stereo enhancement is the sound of Toscanini's gripping reading which reappeared on the U.K. market for two years or so in the early Seventies and has become something of a collector's item. Horvat's recording, although not so widely known, has excellent qualities combined with a budget price.

No. 2 in B, op. 14, "To October" (1927)

Kondrashin—RSFSR Academy Choir—Moscow Philharmonic Orchestra.
(in complete set) HMV SLS 5025; HMV ASD 3060.
(Symphony No. 1) US: Angel S 40236.
Slovak—Slovak Philharmonic Chorus and Orchestra.
(Execution of Stepan Razin) Supraphon SUAST 50958.

The factory whistle called for at one point in the score is replaced in both versions by orchestral brass. Kondrashin's tightly-organised performance, full of vitality and attack, prevents a feeling of diffuseness which can dull the effect of the work. By inflicting discontinuity upon the music by a side-change, Slovak's reading does not wholly avoid this pitfall, but otherwise his performance is first-class.

No. 3 in E flat, op. 20, "May Day" (1929)

Kondrashin—RSFSR Academy Choir—Moscow Philharmonic Orchestra.
(in complete set) HMV SLS 5025; (Symphony No. 1) HMV ASD 3045;
(songs from *Loyalty*) US: Angel S 40245.

An extremely successful reading, sweeping the listener along with its committed atmosphere. The recording copes superbly with Shostakovich's many colours and heavy climaxes, and the chorus and orchestra perform magnificently.

No. 4 in C minor, op. 43 (1935/36)

Kondrashin—Moscow Philharmonic Orchestra.
    (in complete set) HMV SLS 5025; HMV ASD 2741; US: Angel S 40177.
Ormandy—Philadelphia Orchestra.
    CBS Classics 61696; US: Columbia MS 6459.
Previn—Chicago Symphony Orchestra.
    HMV ASD 3440; US: Angel S 37284.

Kondrashin deals bravely with this diffuse work, pulling it into symphonic shape by the sheer force of his musical will. The orchestra seems inspired by his example, and the satisfying result is excellently recorded. Ormandy's performance is less cogent but is a reliable alternative marred only by a side-change in the middle of the Scherzo. Previn's disc avoids this disadvantage in a less than bright but very clear recording in which the conductor's intention seems to be to lighten textures whenever possible. He eschews exaggeration almost everywhere, putting musical restraint before excitement.

No. 5 in D minor, op. 47 (1937)

Ančerl—Czech Philharmonic Orchestra.
    Supraphon SUAST 50052; Music for Pleasure SMFP 2114; US: Vanguard SU 1.
Kertész—Suisse Romande Orchestra.
    Decca Eclipse ECS 767; US: London CS 6327.
Ormandy—Philadelphia Orchestra.
    CBS Classics 61643; US: Columbia MS 7279.
Ormandy—Philadelphia Orchestra.
    UK and US: RCA ARL 1–1149.
Previn—London Symphony Orchestra.
    RCA SB 6651; US: RCA LSC 2866.
Previn—Chicago Symphony Orchestra.
    HMV ASD 3443; US: Angel S 37285.

M. Shostakovich—USSR Symphony Orchestra.
   (in complete set) HMV SLS 5025; HMV ASD 2668; US: Angel S 40163.
Ančerl's sincere reading sounds somewhat dated tonally and there is some phrasing affectation in the Finale, but the performance as a whole gives enormous pleasure. Kertész gives a personal, almost idiosyncratic, reading which still succeeds in conveying much of the work's power and drama. The recording (1962) still sounds full and clear. Although not as exciting as some, Ormandy's earlier (CBS/Columbia) performance is sane and reliable, with solidly musical qualities. His RCA re-make has similar attributes, but doubt surrounds some of the brass playing in the Finale. Previn's high-powered RCA version has excitement and drama but the Finale is taken too fast to allow the structure to stand firm. In this respect his later reading with the Chicago Symphony Orchestra is much more satisfactory. Though one of the closest interpreters to the ultimate authority, Maxim Shostakovich gives a strongly personal reading, departing vastly from the letter of the score. Despite this, the result is characterful and utterly satisfying.

No. 6 in B minor, op. 54* (1939)

Boult—London Philharmonic Orchestra.
   UK and US: Everest SDBR 3007.
Kondrashin—Moscow Philharmonic Orchestra.
   (in complete set) HMV SLS 5025; (Violin Concerto No. 2) HMV ASD
   2447; US: Angel S 40064.
Mravinsky—Leningrad Philharmonic Orchestra.
   HMV ASD 2805; US: Angel S 40202.
Previn—London Symphony Orchestra.
   HMV ASD 3029; US: Angel S 37026.
A two-sided Sixth seems extravagant but, despite relaxed tempi in the first movement, Boult offers beautiful playing and a finely-balanced performance. Also well played, Kondrashin's performance nevertheless lacks conviction, falling back for its effect on superficial excitement. Mravinsky's concert performance (Moscow, 1965) lacks the definition of a studio performance and is marked by audience noise, but the performance is so personal and spontaneous that the listener is carried along by its power. A slow first movement shows Previn in deeply committed mood, contrasting strongly with the sparkling Finale. Only in the middle movement does the reading seem to lack concentration.

---

* Due to a copying error the work was originally listed as op. 53.

No. 7 in C, op. 60 (1941)

Ančerl—Czech Philharmonic Orchestra.
    Rediffusion Heritage HCN 8003 (M); US: Everest SDBR 3404 (M) (2 discs).
Berglund—Bournemouth Symphony Orchestra.
    HMV SLS 897 (2 discs).
Svetlanov—USSR Symphony Orchestra.
    (in complete set) HMV SLS 5025; US: Angel S 4107 (2 discs).
Toscanini—NCB Symphony Orchestra.
    (Symphony No. 1) UK: RCA Victrola VICS 6038 (2 discs).
Ančerl's fine mono recording is compressed on only two sides (a playing time of over sixty-eight minutes without detectable loss of quality) in Rediffusion's bargain Heritage series. Although over two decades old, the sound is more than adequate, and the performance is compelling. Berglund's provincial English orchestra shows itself to be in the top international league, and the Finnish conductor leads the music firmly and with insight. Svetlanov's is also a splendid performance, outshining Berglund's only in the authentic spirit of the playing and the instrumental timbres. Toscanini's performance has unique historical significance, being a recording of the very first public concert of the work outside Russia (July 19, 1942), a concert that was broadcast, amid much publicity, to the American people. The studio stereo production is unobtrusive and helps to tame the rather harsh recording.

No. 8 in C minor, op. 65 (1943)

Kondrashin—Moscow Philharmonic Orchestra.
    (in complete set) HMV SLS 5025; HMV ASD 2474; US: Angel S 40237.
Previn—London Symphony Orchestra.
    HMV ASD 2917; US: Angel S 36980.
Personal preference may well decide which of these two performances is the more satisfying. Both conductors display structural awareness amid the composer's vast time-scales, and if Previn seems more relaxed in parts of the first movement, Kondrashin draws less than the ultimate terror from the famous "shell-fire" movement. Both recordings are excellent, but there is yet room for a version that will do justice to the strength and grandeur of this brooding masterpiece.

No. 9 in E flat, op. 70 (1945)

Horvat—Zagreb Philharmonic Orchestra.
　(Symphony No. 1) Turnabout TV 34223.
Kondrashin—Moscow Philharmonic Orchestra.
　(in complete set) HMV SLS 5025; (Execution of Stepan Razin) HMV ASD
　2409; US: Angel S 40000.
Koussevitzky—Boston Symphony Orchestra.
　RCA Victrola VCM 6174.
Kurtz—New York Philharmonic Orchestra.
　Philips ABL 3117 (M); US: Columbia ML 4137 (M).
Sargent—London Symphony Orchestra.
　UK and US: Everest SDBR 3054.
Kondrashin's free, almost elastic, view tends to distort the lightweight music
by attempting to increase its significance. It is, perhaps, a valid view but not
one for everyday enjoyment despite fine playing. Kurtz's pioneering mono
recording (1950) has admirable clarity and the poise of the performance,
apart from an unusually slow Moderato, brings many delights. Sargent, in an
often under-rated performance gives a well-measured reading with carefully-
judged tempi, the performance being strong enough to outweigh the dis-
advantages of an ageing recording. Koussevitzky's old performance (originally
issued on 78 rpm discs Victor 11–9634/6) shows a fine balance in the
notoriously difficult relation between fast and slow sections of the symphony,
and Horvat's, almost as good in this respect, has the advantage of clear
modern recorded sound.

No. 10 in E minor, op. 93 (1953)

Ančerl—Czech Philharmonic Orchestra.
　Heliodor 478412 (M); US: Decca DL 9822 (M).
Berglund—Bournemouth Symphony Orchestra.
　HMV Greensleeve ESD 7049; US: Angel S 37280.
A. Davis—London Philharmonic Orchestra.
　Classics for Pleasure CFP 40216; US: Seraphim S 60255.
Haitink—London Philharmonic Orchestra.
　Decca SXL 6838; US: London CS 7061.
Karajan—Berlin Philharmonic Orchestra.
　UK and US: DG 139020.
Svetlanov—USSR Symphony Orchestra.
　(in complete set) HMV SLS 5025; HMV ASD 2420; US: Angel S 40025.
Ancerl's mono recording may have been surpassed tonally but his gripping
and superbly-played reading still competes with modern productions. Berg-
lund's is a wholly excellent performance, intense and powerful. Andrew

Davis's version has many fine points but in comparison with others it lacks variety, particularly in the inflection of the horn calls in the third movement. Karajan, in a taut and earnest performance, generates almost unbearable excitement, especially in the Finale. For sheer brilliance his performance is unsurpassed. Svetlanov's, on the other hand, lacks Karajan's personal involvement but is reliable and beautifully played. The first in Haitink's projected complete recording of all the symphonies, the Tenth emerges as immensely well detailed and finely moulded, but its coolness reduces some of the emotional appeal of the music. It augurs well for the cycle, however, and the recording is magnificent.

No. 11 in G minor, op. 103, "The Year 1905" (1957)

Cluytens—French National Radio Orchestra.
    Columbia CX 1604—CXS 1605 (M); US: Angel 3586 3S/L (M).
Kondrashin—Moscow Philharmonic Orchestra.
    (in complete set) HMV SLS 5025; HMV ASD 3010; US: Angel S 40244.
Stokowski—Houston Symphony Orchestra.
    US: Seraphim S 60228.
Cluytens's admirable reading, recorded in the composer's presence in summer 1958 in Paris, was apparently not made in stereo; however, it is still worth attention as the performance would seem to approach closer to the composer's intention than any other on disc. Leopold Stokowski, who also recorded the work in 1958 (in stereo), has divided critics into two camps: those who feel that the recording lacked power, thus depriving his reading of impact, and those who find his presentation of the work's subtle colours, particularly in the Finale, to be unequalled. If for no other reason than to solve this dichotomy of opinion, a new and wholly satisfying version of the work would be welcome. Kondrashin's well-recorded version, with some uncomfortable artificiality in the recorded balance, detracts from the composer's unusually expanded time-scales by the use of often over-fast tempi. A wholly fine performance in good stereo sound is awaited.

No. 12 in D minor, op. 112, "The Year 1917" (1961)

Durjan—Leipzig Gewandhaus Orchestra.
    Philips 6580012.
Mravinsky—Leningrad Philharmonic Orchestra.

(in complete set) HMV SLS 5025; (*The Sun Shines over the Motherland*)
HMV ASD 2598; US: Angel S 40128.

*Durjan's breathtakingly firm grasp of structure and the superb playing and
recording transform this dubiously-conceived work into a major symphonic
utterance. This is one of the most stimulating recordings of Shostakovich's
symphonies so far issued. Mravinsky's too-overt patriotism and apparent
anxiety to convey the "message" of the work detracts from the value of his
performance. This overstatement becomes embarrassing and the recording, by
being brash, abets the effect.*

No. 13 in B flat minor, op. 113, "Babi Yar" (1962)

Kondrashin—Gromadsky (bass)—Moscow Philharmonic Male Chorus and
Orchestra.
    UK and US: Everest SDBR 3181.
Kondrashin—Eisen (bass)—RSFSR Academy Choir—Moscow Philharmonic
Orchestra.
    (in complete set) HMV SLS 5025; HMV ASD 2893; US: Angel S 40212.
Ormandy—Krause (baritone)—Male Chorus of the Mendelssohn Club, Phil-
adelphia—Philadelphia Orchestra.
    RCA SB 6830; US: RCA LSC 3162; (Symphonies Nos. 14 and 15) US:
    RCA CRL 3–1284.

*The first version of the symphony, heard in the earlier Kondrashin perform-
ance (with Gromadsky) and in Ormandy's recording, was never approved by
the authorities: the Everest disc is of a "pirated" recording, while Ormandy's
is presumably a reading of the "pirated" score. Of these two, Kondrashin's
soloist is placed too prominently in relation to the orchestra and the recording
in general is only moderately good, while Ormandy receives first-class recording for his perceptive performance. The use of a less-than-wholly-idiomatic
baritone soloist only slightly detracts from the value of his record. The
revised version may be heard on Kondrashin's Melodiya/HMV disc, a musically
and dramatically convincing reading in which, however, Eisen lacks the
commanding power of Gromadsky. In translation, the offending verses ran:*
I feel myself as a Jew. / Here I tramp across ancient Egypt. / Here I die,
nailed to the Cross; / Even now my hands and feet bear the nail scars. /
I become a titanic silent scream / Over the thousands of graves here. / I am
every old man shot dead here— / I am each child shot dead here. / Nothing
in me will ever forget this. *In the revised version, Yevtushenko changed these
lines to read:* Here I stand as if at the fountainhead / That gives me faith
in our brotherhood. / Here Russians lie, and Ukrainians / Lie together with
Jews in the same ground. / I think of Russia's heroic deed / In blocking the
way to Fascism. / To the infinitesimal dewdrop she is close / To me with her
very being and her fate. / Nothing in me will ever forget this.

No. 14, op. 135 (1969)

Barshay—Miroshnikova (soprano)—Vladimirov (bass)—Moscow Chamber Orchestra.
   (in complete set) HMV SLS 5025; HMV ASD 2633; US: Angel S 40147.
Ormandy—Curtin (soprano)—Estes (bass)—Philadelphia Orchestra.
   RCA LSB 5002; US: RCA LSC 3206; (Symphonies Nos. 13 and 15)
   US: RCA CRL 3–1284.
Rostropovich—Vishnyevskaya (soprano)—Reshetin (bass)—Moscow Philharmonic Orchestra.
   HMV ASD 3090; US: Columbia/Melodiya M 34507.
Barshay gave the first performance (with the soloists on Rostropovich's disc) and here produces a fine interpretation based on deep knowledge. His soloists, despite too prominent balancing, sound effective and refined, possibly too refined for some of the subject-matter, and the recording has a natural, open acoustic. Ormandy's excellent production is unfairly outclassed by the crushing competition of the two Russian versions. He scores, however, in the matter of recording, in which the voices are more naturally balanced vis-à-vis the orchestra. Vishnyevskaya and Reshetin gave the first performance of the work (under Barshay in 1969), but authenticity is not the only value of this thrilling performance. Vishnyevskaya perhaps overdoes the histrionics at times, but Reshetin is unfailingly musical and exciting. Rostropovich remains unsurpassed in this music, and the recording, while unduly emphasising the voices, is beautifully clear and pleasing.

No. 15 in A, op. 141 (1971)

Ormandy—Philadelphia Orchestra.
   UK and US: RCA ARL 1–0014; (Symphonies Nos. 13 and 14) US: RCA CRL 3–1284 (3 discs).
M. Shostakovich—Moscow Radio Symphony Orchestra.
   (in complete set) HMV SLS 5025; (String Quartet No. 11) HMV ASD 2857; US: Angel S 40213.
Choice between these recordings must rely on personal taste. Both are first class in every way, the composer's son perhaps being the more authentic but yielding slightly to Ormandy in the matter of recorded sound. The quadraphonic version of the RCA disc (UK and US: ARD 1–0014) is less satisfactory than the standard stereo pressing when played on twin-channel equipment. In the HMV complete set the second side is filled up with a suite from the Age of Gold music.

Comparative Chart of Contemporary Symphonies

It will not have escaped the notice of readers that Shostakovich was perforce aware of political and military events. In addition to setting his symphonies in their world-wide symphonic context, the following chart indicates the chronological relationship between, for example, the Leningrad Symphony and other "war" and/or "city" symphonies: Polovinkin's "Moscow" (No. 2, 1931), Knipper's "Far Eastern Army" (No. 3, 1933), Polovinkin's "The Red Army" (No. 4, 1933), Mokrussov's "Anti-Fascist" and Stanislav's "Red Army" (both 1942), Karayev's "In Memory of the Heroes of the Great Fatherland War" (No. 1, 1943), Doubrava's "Stalingrad" (No. 2, 1944), Tikotsky's "Liberation of Byelorussia" (No. 3, 1945), Woytowicz's "Warsaw" (No. 2, 1945), Stevens's "Symphony of Liberation" (1945), Muradeli's "War of Liberation" (No. 2, 1947), Farkas's "In Memoriam 4.IV.1945" (1952), and Gabichvadze's "Rostocker" (No. 3, 1975).

Also, other "hero" symphonies may be seen in relation to Shostakovich's plans for a Lenin Symphony: Robert Russell Bennett's "Abraham Lincoln" (1930), Kabalevsky's "Requiem for Lenin" (No. 3) and Shebalin's "Lenin" (No. 3, both 1934), Giannini's "In Memory of Theodore Roosevelt" (No. 1, 1935), Muradeli's "In Memory of Kirov" (No. 1, 1938), Mossolov's "To Lermontov" (No. 4, 1941), Ben Weber's "William Blake" (1952), Jones's "In Memoriam Dylan Thomas" (No. 4, 1954), R. R. Bennett's "Stephen Foster" (No. 4, 1959), and Kancheli's "In Memory of Michelangelo Buonarotti" (No. 4, 1975).

Two "revolution symphonies" should also be noted: Shaporin's "Ode to Revolution" (1933), and Válek's "Revolutionary" (No. 11, 1974).

Abbreviations used for countries of origin are as follows: (Arg) Argentinian; (Arm) Armenian; (Aus) Austria; (Az) Azerbaidzhanian; (Bel) Belgian; (Boh) Bohemian; (Br) Brazilian; (Bul) Bulgarian; (Cro) Croatian; (Cz) Czech; (Da) Danish; (Est) Estonian; (Fin) Finnish; (Fr) French; (G) German; (Geo) Georgian; (Gk) Greek; (Hu) Hungarian; (I) Icelandic; (Is) Israeli; (It) Italian; (Jp) Japanese; (Mex) Mexican; (Ned) Netherlands; (No) Norwegian; (Po) Polish; (Rom) Romanian; (Sib) Siberian; (Sl) Slovak; (Su) Swiss; (Sw) Swedish; (Uk) Ukrainian; (Yu) Yugoslavian.

Year	Shostakovich	Other Russian	Eastern European	American	British	Others
1920			Enesco No.3 (Rom) Kósa No.1 (Hu)	Converse No.2 Becker No.2		Chávez No.1 (Mex) Villa-Lobos No.5 (Br)
1921			Kvapil No.2 (Cz) Ragowski No.1 (Po)			Bengtsson No.3 (Sw) Křenek No.1 (Aus) Pijper No.2 (Ned) Roussel No.2 (Fr)
1922		Myaskovsky Nos. 6 and 7 Roslavets Symphony	Suda Symphony (Cz) Zádor No.1 (Hu)	Converse No.3 Kelly No.1	Bax No.1 Bliss "A Colour Symphony" Brian No.1 Vaughan Williams No.3	Atterberg No.5 (Sw) Milhaud Nos.4 and 5 (Fr) Nielsen No.5 (Da)
1923			Wiłkomirski Symphony (Po)	Hanson No.1	Dunhill Symphony Wood No.2	Sibelius No.6 (Fin)
1924		Prokofiev No.2	Jirák No.2 (Cz) Řidký No.1 (Cz) Laks Symphony (Po)	Saminsky No.3	Holst "Choral Symphony"	Sibelius No.7 (Fin) Baeyens No.1 (Bel)
1925	No.1	Myaskovsky Nos. 9 and 10 Shebalin No.1	Perkowski No.1 (Po) Řidký No.2 (Cz)	Copland No.1 Antheil "Jazz Symphony"	Bax No.2 Britten "Simple Symphony"	Beck No.1 (Su) Nielsen No. 6 (Da)

	Shostakovich	Other Russian	Eastern European	American	British	Others
1926		Kastalsky "Symphony of the Tilling of the Soil"	Andricu Chamber Symphony No.1 (Rom) Szelényi No.1 (Hu)	Antheil No.1		Madetoja No.3 (Fin) Pijper No.3 (Ned) Saeverud No.3 (No)
1927	No.2	Knipper No.1 Cherepnin No.1	Bořkovec No.1 (Cz) Karel No.3 (Cz)	Sessions No.1 Shepherd No.1	Boughton No.2 Walford-Davies No.2	Atterberg No.6 (Sw) Baeyens No.3 (Bel)
1928		Mossolov No.1 Prokofiev No.3	Řídký Nos.3 and 4 (Cz)	Copland No.2 Thomson No.1	Bantock No.3	Larsson No.1 (Sw) Webern Symphony (Aus)
1929		Lopatnikov No.1 Shebalin No.2	Foerster No. 5 (Cz)	Becker No.3 Thompson No.1	Bax No.3 Jacob No.1	Rangstrom No.3 (Sw) Beck No.4 (Su)
1930		Prokofiev No.4 Stravinsky "Symphony of Psalms"	Kósa No.2 (Hu) Krejčí "Vocal Symphony" (Cz) Rózsa Symphony (Hu)	Bennett No.1 Hanson No.2 Still No.1	Bliss "Morning Heroes"	Honegger No.1 (Sui) Roussel No.3 (Fr)
1931	No.3	Brussilovsky No.1 Polovinkin No.2	Kondracki No.1 (Po) Nejedlý No.1 (Cz)	Thomson No.2 Thompson No.2	Bax No.4	Ibert No.1 (Fr) Nystroem No.1 (Sw)

	Shostakovich	Other Russian	Eastern European	American	British	Others
1932		Kabalevsky No.1 Myaskovsky Nos. 11 and 12 Knipper No.2	Martinů Symphony for two orchestras (Cz) Szymanowski No.4 (Po)	Still No.2 Saminsky No.5	Lloyd No.1	Badings No.2 (Ned) Castro No.1 (Arg)
1933		Myaskovsky Nos. 13 and 14 Knipper No.3 Polovinkin No.4 Shaporin Symphony	Frid Symphony (Hu) Řídký No.5 (Cz)	Copland No.3 Harris No.1	Lloyd Nos. 2 and 3	Chávez No.2 (Mex) Rosenberg No.2 (Sw) Weill No.2 (G)
1934		Ippolitov-Ivanov No.2 Kabalevsky Nos. 2 and 3 Khachaturyan No.1 (Arm) Myaskovsky No.15 Shebalin No.3	Kósa No.4 (Hu) Kubelík No.1 (Cz) Novák No.1	Harris No.2 Porter No.1	Bax Nos. 5 and 6 Morris Symphony	Badings No.3 (Ned) Hindemith "Mathis der Maler" (G) Malipiero No.4 (It) Roussel No.4 (Fr) Strauss Symphony for wind (G)
1935		Khrennikov No.1 Shebalin No.4	Axman No.5 (Cz) Folprecht No.1 (Cz) Švara No.2 (Yu)	Schuman No.1 Giannini No.1	Vaughan Williams No.4 Walton No.1	Holmboe No.1 (Da) Schönberg Chamber Symphony No.1 (Aus)
1936	No.4	Myaskovsky No.16 Rakhmaninov No.3	Lajtha No.1 (Hu) Folprecht No.2 (Cz) Kósa No.5 (Hu)	Barber No.1 (original) Gould No.1 Hovhaness No.1	Rubbra No.1 Wordsworth Symphony	Chávez No.3 (Mex) Larsson No.2 (Sw) Martinon No.1 (Fr) Rangström No.4 (Sw)

Year	Shostakovich	Other Russian	Eastern European	American	British	Others
1937	No.5	Myaskovsky Nos. 17 and 18 Mossolov No.3	Jora Symphony (Rom) Kubelík Symphony (Cz)	Harris No.3 Piston No.1 Schuman No.2 Varèse Symphony	Moeran Symphony Boughton No.3	Saeverud No.4 (No) Toch No.1 (G)
1938		Avshalomov No.1 (Sib) Knipper No.6 Lopatnikov No.2 Muradeli No.1 (Geo)	Karel No.4 (Cz) Řídký No.6 (Cz)	Cowell No.2 Shepherd No.2	Gibbs No.2	Barraine No.2 (Fr) Brun No.8 (Su)
1939	No.6	Myaskovsky No.19 Revutsky No.2 (Uk)	Kisielewski Symphony (Po)	Cadman Symphony	Bax No.7 Rubbra No.3	Milhaud No.1 (Fr) Rosenberg No.3 (Sw) Wirén No.2 (Sw) Pfitzner No.2 (G)
1940		Myaskovsky Nos. 20 and 21 Sviridov No.1	Pipkov No.1 (Bul) Rogowski No.3 (Po) Šatra No.2 (Cz)	Converse No.5 Creston No.1 Diamond No.1 Gillis Nos.1 and 2	Bantock No.4 Berkeley No.1 Britten "Sinfonia da Requiem" Goossens No.1	Casella No.3 (It) Hartmann No.1 (G) Stravinsky Symphony in C (Fr) Pfitzner No.3 Schönberg Chamber Symphony No.2 (Aus)
1941	No.7	Myaskovsky Nos. 22 and 23 Mossolov No.4	Kremenliev Symphony (Bul) Moyzes No.2 (Sl)	Gillis No.3 Hanson No.3 Schuman Nos. 3 and 4 B. Herrmann Symphony		Hindemith No.2 (G) Honegger No.2 (Su) Saeverud No.5 (No)

Year	Shostakovich	Other Russian	Eastern European	American	British	Others
1942		Khachaturyan No.2 (Arm) Khrennikov No.2 Mokrussov Symphony Stanislav Symphony	Kabeláč No.1 (Cz) Kadosa No.1 (Hu) Kardoš No.1 (Sl) Martinů No.1 (Cz)	Bergsma Chamber Symphony Bernstein No.1 Cowell No.3 Harris No.5 Mennin No.1	Rubbra No.4 Gipps No.1	Saeverud No.6 (No) Alfvén No.5 (Sw)
1943		Grechaninov No.6 Knipper No.8 Myaskovsky No.24 Karaev No.1 (Az)	Bacewicz No.1 (Po) Dobiáš No.1 (Cz) Kapr No.1 (Cz) Martinů No.2 (Cz)	Barber No.1 (revised) Hanson No.4 Piston No.2 Schuman No.5	Vaughan Williams No.5 Jacob Symphony for strings	Atterberg No.7 (Sw) Blomdahl No.1 (Sw) Leifs Symphony (I)
1944		Hartmann No.2 Prokofiev No.5 Balanchivadze No.1 (Geo)	Martinů No.3 (Cz) Doubrava No.2 (Cz)	Barber No.2 (original) Creston No.2 Foss No.1 Mennin No.2	Goossens No.2 Jacob No.2	Ginastera No.1 (Arg) Rosenberg No.5 (Sw) Villa-Lobos No.6 (Br) Wirén No.3 (Sw)
1945	No.9	Peiko No.1 Tikotsky No.3	Martinů No.4 (Cz) Kubelík No.2 (Cz) Woytowicz No.2 (Po)	Stevens No.1 Still No.3 Stravinsky "Symphony in Three Movements"	Jones No.1 Tippett No.1 Stevens "Symphony of Liberation"	Atterberg No.8 (Sw) Larsson No.3 (Sw) Skalkottas Symphony (Gk) Wellesz No.1 (Aus)
1946		Myaskovsky No.25 Peiko No.2 Karayev No.2 (Az)	Martinů No.5 (Cz) Andrieu No.2 (Rom) Kabeláč No.2 (Cz)	Blitzstein "Airborne Symphony" Copland No.4 Diamond No.5 Gould No.4 Mennin No.3	Arnold Symphony for strings Lloyd No.4	Honegger Nos.3 and 4 (Su) Milhaud No.3 (Fr)
1947		Chaykovsky No.1 Khachaturyan No.3 (Arm) Mossolov No.5 Muradeli No.2 (Geo)	Lutosławski No.1 (Po) Burian Symphony (Cz) Moyzes No.4 Krenz Symphony (Po)	Barber No.2 (revised) Gillis No.5½ Piston No.3 Still No.4	Vaughan Williams No.6 Cooke No.1 Mellers No.1	Blomdahl No.2 (Sw) Fernström No.11 (Sw) Henze No.1 (G)

Year	Shostakovich	Other Russian	Eastern European	American	British	Others
1948		Avshalomov No.2 (Sib) Myaskovsky No.26	Kadosa No.2 (Hu) Lajtha No.3 (Hu)	Mennin No.4 Schuman No.6	Lloyd No.5 Maconchy No.1 Willan No.2	Blomdahl No.3 (Sw) Hartmann No.3 (G) Henze No.2 (G) Messiaen "Turangalîla Symphony" (Fr)
1949		Avshalomov No.3 (Sib) Myaskovsky No.27 Prokofiev No.6 Taktakishvili No.1(Geo)	Panufnik No.1 (Po) Andricu No.3 (Rom)	Bernstein No.2 Piston No.4 Antheil No.6 Thompson No.3	Brian No.8 Britten "Spring Symphony" Bush No.2 Fricker No.1	Bentzon No.4 (Da) Henze No.3 (G) Křenek No.5 (Aus)
1950		Amirov No.2 (Az)	Bacewicz No.2 (Po) Baird No.1 (Po) Moyzes No.6 (Sl)	Creston No.3 Rorem No.1 Schuller No.1 Stevens No.1 (revised)	Rawsthorne No.1 Alwyn No.1	Korngold Symphony (Aus) Villa-Lobos No.8 (Br) Wellesz No.4 (Aus)
1951		Karetnikov No.1 Cherepnin No.2 Arakishvili No.3 (Geo)	Lajtha No.4(Hu) Ilev No.2 (Bul)	Creston No.4 Gould No.5 H. Herrmann No.4 Mennin No.5	Brian No.9 Simpson No.1	Hindemith Nos.3 and 4 (G) Honegger No.5 (Su) Malipiero No.12 (It)
1952		Prokofiev No.7 Cherepnin No.3	Bacewicz No.3 (Po) Farkas Symphony (Hu) Hanuš No.2 (Cz)	Bloch No.3 Weber Symphony	Arnold No.1 Berkeley No.2	Bentzon No.7 (Da) Chávez No.5 (Mex) Holmboe No.8 (Da) Pettersson No.2 (Sw) Wirén No.4 (Sw)
1953	No.10	Taktakishvili No.2 (Geo)	Husa Symphony (Cz) Nikolov No.1 (Bul) Serocki No.2 (Po)	Mennin No.6 Cowell Nos. 9 and 10	Arnold No.2 Vaughan Williams "Sinfonia Antartica" Mellers No.2	Badings No.6 (Ned) David "Sinfonia Praeclassica" (Aus) Toch No.3 (G) Jolivet No.1 (Fr)

	Shostakovich	Other Russian	Eastern European	American	British	Others
1954		Lopatnikov No.3 Prigozhin No.1 Schwartz No.1	Enesco "Chamber Symphony" (Rom) Martinů No.6 (Cz)	Cowell No.11 Piston No.5	Jones No.4 Rubbra No.6	Badings No.7 (Ned) Akutagawa No.1 (Jp)
1955		Ustvolskaya No.1	Bořkovec No.2 (Cz) Havelka No.1 (Cz)	Creston No.5 Hanson No.5 H. Herrmann No.5 Piston No.6	Hoddinott No.1	Henze No.4 (G) Ibert No.2 (Fr) Toch Nos.4 and 5 (G)
1956		Kabalevsky No.4	Bartoš No.2 (Cz) Josif No.1 (Yu)	Hovhaness No.3	Simpson No.2 Vaughan Williams No.8	Atterberg No.9 (Sw) Badings No.8 (Ned)
1957	No.11	Cherepnin No.4 Peiko No.3 Balanchivadze No.2 (Geo)	Dobiáš No.2 (Cz) Doráti Symphony (Hu) Rääts No.1 (Est)	McPhee No.2 Rorem No.3 Stevens No.2 Sessions No.3	Arnold No.3 Rubbra No.7	Beck No.7 (Su) Milhaud No.8 (Fr) Villa-Lobos No.12 (Br)
1958		Arutunyan Symphony (Arm) Shchedrin No.1	Kabeláč No.4 (Cz) Andricu No.7 (Rom)	Sessions No.4 Cowell No.13	Tippett No.2 Vaughan Williams No.9 Searle No.2	Akutagawa No.3 (Jp) Berger No.4 (Aus)
1959		Eshpay No.1 Karetnikov No.3	Bořkovec No.3 (Cz) Kadosa No.4 (Hu)	Bennett No.4 Hovhaness Nos.4, 6 and 7	Rawsthorne No.2 Alwyn No.4	Egge No.3 (No) Jolivet No.2 (Fr) Saeverud No.8 (No)

	Shostakovich	Other Russian	Eastern European	American	British	Others
1960		Yegiazaryan Symphony (Arm)	Andricu No.8 (Rom) Doubrava No.4 (Cz)	Schuman No.7 Hovhaness No.11 (original)	Arnold No.4 Brian Nos.14, 15 and 16 Bush No.3 Walton No.2	Einem Symphony (G) Kokkonen No.1 (Fin) Milhaud Nos.10 and 11 (Fr)
1961	No.12	Beglarian Symphony (Geo) Vaynberg No.4	Kadosa No.5 (Hu) Kalabis No.2 (Cz) Kodály Symphony (Hu)	Piston No.7 Yardumian No.1	Arnold No.5 Lloyd No.8	Jolivet No.3 (Fr) Kokkonen No.2 (Fin)
1962	No.13	Chaykovsky No.2 Eshpay No.2 Vaynberg No.5	Andricu No.9 and Chamber Symphony No.2 (Rom) Eller No.3 (Est)	Cowell No.16 Schuman No.8 Hovhaness Nos.15 and 16	Maxwell Davies No.1 Simpson No.3 Searle No.4	Hartmann No.8 (G) Henze No.5 (G)
1963		Karetnikov No.4 Vaynberg No.6	Kardoš No.5 (Sl) Lajtha No.9 (Hu) Panufnik No.3 (Po)	Bernstein No.3 Hovhaness Nos.17 and 18	Britten "Cello Symphony" Goehr "Little Symphony"	Bentzon No.10 (Da) Henze No.1 (revised) (G) Nystroem No.5 (Sw) Toch No.6 (G)
1964		Irino No.2	Barati Symphony (Hu) Flosman Symphony (Cz) Petrovics Symphony (Yu) Schäffer No.2 (Po)	Mennin No.7 Cowell Nos.18 and 19 Sessions No.5	Rawsthorne No.3 Jones No.6 Searle No.5	Badings No.12 (Ned) Jolivet No.4 (Fr) Milhaud No.13 (Fr) Toch No.7 (G) Ginastera No.2 (Arg)

Year	Shostakovich	Other Russian	Eastern European	American	British	Others
1965		Shchedrin No.2 Peiko No.4	Bartoš No.3 (Cz) Bentoiu Symphony (Bul)	Cowell No.20 Piston No.8 Schuller No.2	Bennett No.1 Brian No.22 McCabe No.1 Mathias No.1	David No.8 (Aus) Martinon No.4 (Fr) Nystroem No.6 (Sw) Saeverud No.9 (No)
1966		Eshpay No.3 Tishchenko No.3	Kadosa No.6 (Hu) Pärt No.2 (Est) Podesva No.3 (Cz)	Sessions No.6 Hovhaness No.19	Fricker No.4 Maw Symphony	Pettersson No.6 (Sw) Avidom No.8 (Is)
1967		Banshchikov Symphony Ustvolskaya No.2	Lutoslawski No.2 (Po) Anhalt "Symphony of Modules" (Hu) Feld No.1 (Cz) Rääts No.6 (Est)	Diamond No.9 Gillis No.10 Sessions No.7	Arnold No.6 Bennett No.2 Brian No.30	Pettersson No.7 (Sw) Egge No.4 (No)
1968		Karetnikov No.5	Bartoš No.4 (Cz) Kapr No.8 (Cz) Válek No.5 (Cz) Baird No.3 (Po)	Hanson No.6 Schuman No.9 Sessions No.8	Rubbra No.8 Knussen No.1 Walker Nos.5 and 6	Kokkonen No.3 (Fin) Rosenberg No.7 (Sw) Wellesz No.7 (Aus)
1969		Falik Symphony Peiko No.5	Barta No.2 (Cz) Kadosa No.8 (Hu) Válek No.6 (Cz)	Harris No.12 Hovhaness No.11 (revised) Perry No.8	Berkeley No.3 Williamson No.2	Egge No.5 (No) Henze No.6 (G)

	Shostakovich	Other Russian	Eastern European	American	British	Others
1970	No.14	Tsytovich Symphony	Kabeláč No.8 (Cz) Válek No.7 (Cz) Goleminov No.3 (Bul)	Hovhaness No.22	Goehr No.2	Holmboe No.10 (Da) Malipiero No.17 (It) Wellesz No.8 (Aus)
1971	No.15		Kalabis No.3 (Cz) Válek Nos.8 and 9 (Cz)	Persichetti No.9 Siegmeister No.5	McCabe No.2 Tippett No.3	Bucht No.7 (Sw) Holmboe No.10 (Da)
1972			Raichev No.5 (Bul) Sakac Symphony (Cro)	Hovhaness No.23	Jones Nos.7 and 8	Pettersson No.10 (Sw) Lundsten Nordic Nature Symphony No.1 (No)
1973			Penderecki Symphony (Po) Válek No.10 (Cz) Tzvetanov No.3 (Bul)	Hovhaness Nos.24 and 25	Hoddinott No.5 Alwyn No.5	Pettersson No.12 (Sw)
1974			Válek No.11 (Cz) Vacek Symphony (Cz)		Arnold No.7 Jones No.9 Rubbra No.10	
1975		Kancheli No.4 (Geo)	Gabichvadze No.3 (Bul) Lang No.2 (Hu) Tausinger "Sinfonia Bohemica" (Boh)	Hovhaness No.26 Cooper No.4		Lundsten Nordic Nature Symphony No.2 (No) Rihm No.2 (G)

Index of Shostakovich's Works

String Quartets

Vocal

General Index

The prefix "R" to a page number against a conductor's name refers to a performance by that artist listed in the Recommended Recordings section.